Hearing Spiritual Voices

Hearing Spiritual Voices

Medieval Mystics, Meaning and Psychiatry

Christopher C.H. Cook

t&tclark

LONDON • NEW YORK • OXFORD • NEW DELHI • SYDNEY

T&T CLARK
Bloomsbury Publishing Plc
50 Bedford Square, London, WC1B 3DP, UK
1385 Broadway, New York, NY 10018, USA
29 Earlsfort Terrace, Dublin 2, Ireland

BLOOMSBURY, T&T CLARK and the T&T Clark logo are trademarks of
Bloomsbury Publishing Plc

First published in Great Britain 2023

A catalogue record for this book is available from the British Library.

A catalog record for this book is available from the Library of Congress.

ISBN: HB: 978-0-5677-0798-7
         PB: 978-0-5677-0797-0
         ePDF: 978-0-5677-0800-7
         eBook: 978-0-5677-0799-4

Typeset by Integra Software Services Pvt. Ltd.
Printed and bound in Great Britain

To find out more about our authors and books visit www.bloomsbury.com
and sign up for our newsletters.

CONTENTS

ACKNOWLEDGEMENTS

I began writing about Margery Kempe, Julian of Norwich and Joan of Arc during the first phase (2012–15) of the Hearing the Voice project at Durham University. This book was finally completed only after the end of the second phase (2015–22). During the course of the ten years in which I worked on this project, I learned an enormous amount from many colleagues at Durham University and further afield, especially during Friday afternoon meetings of Voice Club, all of which has contributed to the thinking that underlies my writing here. I would especially like to thank Charles Fernyhough (principal investigator for the project) and my fellow co-investigators Angela Woods, Ben Alderson-Day, Corinne Saunders and Pat Waugh. Charles, Corinne and Angela have kindly read various drafts of parts of the manuscript at different stages of its evolution, and I am indebted to them for their comments. I am grateful to Wellcome Trust for their generous funding of both phases of the project, without which this book would not have been possible (grant numbers WT098455MA and 108720/Z/15/Z). Wellcome have also provided funding so that this book can be available on an open-access basis.

More widely, my thinking about this topic has been influenced by those who have generously shared with me their experiences of hearing spiritually significant voices (references to which research are included at the end of this book) and by my students, especially Nathan White, whose PhD research on Julian provided the opportunity for many stimulating conversations over coffee in Durham. My thinking about the clinical implications, and about the relationships between spirituality and psychiatry more widely, has been informed by colleagues at the Spirituality and Psychiatry Special Interest Group at the Royal College of Psychiatrists. Reflections on the interdisciplinary issues and on the location of this material within the wider field of the critical medical humanities owe much to my colleagues at the Institute for Medical Humanities at Durham University.

As always, I am grateful to my family and friends for their support along the way, and to my spiritual director who periodically asks me what I think God is saying to me. These conversations remind me that there are many ways in which God may be said to speak to us, many of which do not involve voices, as they are visual, ineffable or silent, and that this book only explores a small part of a much wider field of spiritual experience.

Finally, I am grateful to Anna Turton and colleagues at Bloomsbury for all of their support during the preparation and production of this book.

CHRONOLOGY

Year	Europe	England		Julian	Margery	France		Joan
1327								
1328		Edward III				Philip VI		
1342				Birth				
1346	Black Death							
1350								
1353						John II		
1364								
1373				Illness & visions	Birth	Charles V		
1377		Richard II						
1378	Great Schism							
1380								
1381			Peasants' Revolt					
c. 1393				Around this time the long text was written	Marriage to John Kempe; Puerperal illness	Charles VI		
1399								
1409	Council of Pisa	Henry IV						
c. 1412								Birth
1413				Margery visits Julian in Norwich				
1415	Battle of Agincourt	Henry V			Pilgrimage to Holy Land, Assisi & Rome			
c. 1416				Death				
1417					Pilgrimage to Santiago de Compostela		Charles VII named Dauphin	
1420	Treaty of Troyes							
1422								

Year	Europe	England		Julian	Margery	France			Joan
c. 1425									Begins hearing voices
1428	Siege of Orleans							Domrémy burned by the Burgundians	
1429								Dauphin crowned at Reims	Audience with the Dauphin
1430									Captured by the Burgundians
(c)1431		Henry VI			Death of husband and son	Henry VI (claimant)	Charles VII		Trial at Rouen; Burned at the stake
1432					First attempt at writing Book I				
1433					Pilgrimage to Wilsnack & Aachen				
1436					Book I re-written by a priest				
1438					Book II begun				
c. 1440					Death				
1449			Rouen recaptured by Charles VII						
1450									Preliminary inquiry into the Rouen trial
1452									Canonical investigation into the Rouen trial
1453									
1456									Nullification of Rouen trial verdict
1461			Henry VI deposed						

Introduction

Unusual perceptual, or perception-like, experiences, often meaningful to those who have them, may be sympathetically or unsympathetically interpreted by others. One interpretation, especially when voices are associated with unusual behaviour, is that they are evidence of mental disorder. Ostensibly such interpretations are sympathetic (showing concern for someone who is ill), but in practice they are used to deny the meaning and value of the experiences for those concerned, thus depriving them (and others) of creative and innovative ways of understanding the human condition. The question is thus one of meaning. Are such experiences meaningful only as indicators of a diagnosis, or are they meaningful in other ways, shedding light on human self-understanding and perhaps even a wider spiritual reality?

Psychiatry has tended to see such phenomena as diagnostically meaningful but not as sources of deeper insight into the human condition. Even if, in a person-centred approach to psychiatry, it might be conceded that these experiences may have some meaning for the person concerned, they are rarely, if ever, seen to have wider value, or to offer insights from which others may learn. Historically, theologically and anthropologically, this is a rather radical departure. Whilst distinctions have long been made between madness and divine inspiration, with the former likely to be seen as offering a distorted vision of reality, the possibility of genuine revelation through perception-like experiences has generally been held as valid in diverse religions, cultures and historical contexts.

This book will take as its focus of study three late-fourteenth-/early-fifteenth-century examples of women who heard spiritually significant voices: Margery Kempe (*c.* 1373–*c.* 1440), Julian of Norwich (1342–*c.* 1416) and Joan of Arc (*c.* 1412–31). Each of these women, in different ways, had an impact on the world around her. Margery's spirituality was socially controversial, but never shown to be theologically unorthodox. Julian, as an anchoress, appears to have been widely consulted as a wise woman known for her depth of spirituality. Joan gained the ear of the politically powerful and fought alongside men in battle because, as she believed, God had called her to do so. All three women bequeathed an enduring legacy in literature and history. Margery is generally accredited as having left the first autobiography of an English woman. Julian's writings represent the earliest extant work in English by a female author. Joan influenced the course of the Hundred Years' War.

Modern psychiatric commentary on the voices that these women reported has generally focused on diagnosis rather than on wider questions of meaning. These commentaries are, in effect, as much the focus of this study as are Margery, Julian and Joan themselves. Whilst they will be held up more often as an example of what not to do, rather than as helpful examples of good practice, they will also be used as a lens through which to examine contemporary psychiatric practice. It will be the contention of this book that psychiatric practice might be enriched by the humanities and enabled to find a more spiritually empathetic, if not also sympathetic, enriching and meaning-enhancing perspective on unusual mental phenomena.

Margery, Julian and Joan have been selected for study by virtue of the wide influence that they have had in literature and/or history, availability of contemporary textual evidence recording their experiences, an extensive secondary literature and, within this literature, a significant interest in the question of making retrospective diagnoses of their alleged psychiatric disorders. They are, conveniently, more or less, contemporaries of each other within a shared Christian culture of medieval Europe. Margery and Julian both lived in East Anglia; Joan lived in France.

Let us begin by considering briefly what is known of the historical context, the biographies of these three women and the written records that remain as testimony to their experiences.

Historical context

Julian, Margery and Joan lived in troubled times, beset by war, disease and theological dispute.[1]

The Hundred Years' War (1337–1453) began before Julian was born and did not finish until after Margery had died. Lasting more than a hundred years and comprising a series of conflicts rather than a continuous war, it had come about due to the claim of the Norman King of England, Edward III, to be the rightful heir to the French throne (his mother was the daughter of Philippe IV of France). The politics were, however, complicated, to say the least. Since the Norman conquest, dukes of Normandy had also been English kings and had formed an alliance with the dukes of Burgundy. The claim of Edward III to the French throne was disputed on the basis of an obscure and forgotten law. The King of France, Charles VI, suffered recurrent episodes of psychosis, possibly due to porphyria. During one of these episodes, at the Treaty of Troyes (1420), Queen Isabeau agreed a settlement in which the French crown would pass, on her husband's death, not to their son Charles (already referred to as dauphin) but to the heirs of Henry V of England, who was to marry their daughter Catherine.

As if the war was not enough for the people of England and France to contend with, the Black Death (1346–53) devasted Europe during the time of Julian's childhood, killing half the population, and continued to revisit Norwich in further smaller waves in the later part of the fourteenth century. Yet, bubonic plague was – overall – only one of a number of threats to health, and probably not the most serious one amongst many other diseases that were endemic at the time, including various causes of high infant mortality, tuberculosis and a number of other infectious diseases (Robb et al., 2021). Famine, due to poor harvests and disease of cattle, further added to the suffering of ordinary people in England.

The Christian church, which in theory united medieval Europe, also faced its problems. The Great Schism (1378–1417) divided the western church between allegiance to papal claimants in Avignon

---

[1]The brief historical review in this section has been informed by Jantzen (2000, pp. 3–14), Bale (2021), Ramirez (2017), Pernoud (1964) and Tavard (1998), amongst other sources.

and in Rome. The end of the fourteenth century and the beginning of the fifteenth were thus marked by divided ecclesial allegiances, with England generally supporting the Roman pope and France the pope in Avignon. An attempt to resolve this split by way of the Council of Pisa (1409) only resulted in a third contender. At the Council of Constance (1414–18) the abdication of Gregory XII was accepted, John XXIII and Benedict XII were deposed and Martin V was elected, thus bringing the schism to an end in the minds of most people. Despite this, there was continued support in Aragon for Benedict, where he was succeeded in 1424 by antipope Clement VIII, and yet another antipope, styling himself Benedict XIII, emerged in 1425.[2]

Despite its wars, diseases and schisms, Europe was largely united by a common vision of Christian spirituality within which death was mitigated by the theological narrative of the passion of Christ and a hope of participation in his resurrection. Against the backdrop of this common Catholic culture and theology, Lollardy, foreshadowing many of the controversies of the reformation, was – in England – seen as a dangerous threat to orthodoxy. Lollardy, drawing significantly upon the work of John Wyclif, was critical of the power and wealth of the church, emphasizing interior holiness over conformity to church law (Mursell, 2001, pp. 170–4). Widespread anger against both the church and secular authorities in England led to the Peasants' Revolt in 1381, which saw looting and pillaging of monasteries and churches in Norwich and elsewhere at a time when Julian may well have already been an anchoress and Margery was a child. Ecclesiastical authority, not least that of the Bishop of Norwich, was held in low esteem and abuses of such authority were condemned especially by the Lollards.

By the time Julian experienced her visions, the Hundred Years' War had brought England to a point of low morale, although it had also, paradoxically, increased the prosperity of Norwich as a significant port and centre of trade. Norwich, in addition to being a centre for Lollardy, was home to a community of Beguines, a group of women committed to a life of prayer and care for the poor who – despite this – were also suspected of heresy. Bishop's Lynn (now

---

[2]See the helpful footnote by Warner (2013, pp. 280–1), where this is related to questioning of Joan about papal allegiance by the Count of Armagnac (see also pp. 78–9).

King's Lynn), the home of Margery Kempe and also a significant port, was similarly prosperous and had close links to the Baltic and other northern European ports.

The late-fourteenth-century English context of Julian's *Revelations* and Margery's *Book* was thus one of pervasive suffering, poverty and loss of confidence both in church and in state. On the other side of the English Channel, by the early fifteenth century, France was divided. The people of Joan's hometown, Domrémy, appear largely to have taken the side of France, against England and Burgundy, and Joan grew up amidst the fear of hostility, looting and conflict. In 1415, the French had suffered a heavy defeat at Agincourt and in 1418 the English had occupied Paris. At the Treaty of Troyes in 1420, the dauphin was disinherited in favour of the King of England, Henry V. In 1422, Henry unexpectedly died and England and occupied France were ruled firmly by John, Duke of Bedford; whereas the dauphin, pushed back south of the Loire, was generally seen as weak and on the defensive. In this context, Orleans was a strategic military objective, commanding as it did a key bridge across the Loire. Under siege by Thomas Montague, Earl of Salisbury, it must have seemed in October 1428 that it was all but inevitable that Orleans too would fall to the enemy power. Contrary to this, Joan's voices told her that she would raise the siege of Orleans, that she would be instrumental in bringing about the coronation of the dauphin in Rheims and that she would expel her king's enemies.

Margery Kempe

Margery[3] was the daughter of a burgess in King's Lynn who held a number of important positions locally and nationally, including being a member of the parliament (Windeatt, 1994, p. 10). Her marriage to John Kempe in 1393, at the age of twenty years, seems to have represented a drop in social status. Following the birth of their first child she suffered a significant mental illness, lasting about six months, which was resolved following a vision of Jesus,

---

[3]This account of Margery's life draws especially upon Bale (2021, pp. 228–37), Bhattacharji (1997) and Mursell (2001).

who said 'Daughter, why have you forsaken me, and I never forsook you?' (p. 42).[4] After this she suffered the failure of two attempted business ventures, one in brewing and then another in milling. By the time Margery and John had been married for twenty years, they had fourteen children.

Around 1409, her life took a significant turn, sometimes described as a 'conversion', following an experience in which she 'heard a melodious sound so sweet and delectable that she thought she had been in paradise' (p. 46). Margery began to engage in more public displays of religious piety and formed a desire to end sexual relations with her husband. In 1413, she eventually persuaded her husband to allow her to adopt a life of chastity, in exchange for paying off his debts. During the first half of 1413, she made a visit to Julian of Norwich seeking reassurance about the experiences that she was having, including the 'very many holy speeches and converse that our Lord spoke to her soul' in order to 'find out if there were any deception in them' (p. 77). In the latter part of the same year, she set off on pilgrimage to the holy land, returning via Assisi and Rome, reaching England again in 1415. In 1417, she made a pilgrimage to Santiago de Compostela and, following her return home to England, was detained and put on trial in Leicester, then in York, Cawood and Beverly. In each case, she was released without any conviction of heresy or criminal wrongdoing.

In around 1418, she developed an unknown illness which 'settled in her right side', associated with intermittent severe vomiting, which lasted for eight years. The 1420s appear to have been a quiet phase in Margery's life, during which she remained in King's Lynn, but in the early 1430s her husband became ill, probably with some form of dementia, and she nursed him until his death in 1432, following which she made a final pilgrimage to Wilsnack and Aachen.

Although Margery herself was illiterate, around 1432, she recruited the help of an unknown man to write down the story of her religious experiences. In 1436, this task was taken up again by another man, a priest, who wrote Book I. Book II was begun, with the help of the same priest, in 1438.

---

[4]All quotations are taken from Windeatt, 1994, and page numbers refer accordingly to this edition.

We are told in the proem and preface that the first draft of Margery's *Book*, written by someone whose English was limited, and which appears to have been very difficult to read, was revised in 1436. It was not written in chronological order and was mostly written long after the events which it records. It was then lost, apart from a few extracts published in the sixteenth century, until an early copy of the complete book was discovered in 1934 in the personal collection of the Butler-Bowden family (Meech and Allen, 1940).

Margery tells us that her *Book* was written to tell of how Jesus had moved her, a sinful woman, to follow him and seek the way of perfection. To this end, Margery is not afraid to tell of her faults, especially in the earlier chapters of the book. Only after twenty years since she 'first had feelings and revelations' did the book get written, and then because she believed that God had commanded her to do so, in order that 'his goodness might be known to all the world' (p. 35). She refers to herself habitually throughout, in the third person, as 'this creature'. And yet, despite these signs of humility, there is a paradoxical dimension to the *Book* in that, in the process of describing her feelings and revelations and of seeking to show how she has been moved to pursue perfection, she inevitably promotes herself as the one who has been so privileged and so moved. She appears to have modelled herself upon, or at least saw herself as sharing similar experiences with, a variety of other holy women including Bridget of Sweden, Mary d'Oignies and perhaps Angela of Foligno.

Margery was a controversial character in her own time, not least because of her profuse weeping in public, her assumed authority to speak of heavenly matters, her attention-attracting decision to dress in white, her outspokenness and her propensity to antagonize people at all levels of society. And yet she also attracted those who befriended her and who sympathized with her cause. Amidst these ambiguities and tensions, the voices that Margery heard play a significant part in her apologia for her life.

Julian of Norwich

Julian of Norwich was a late-fourteenth-century anchoress who lived in a cell attached to St Julian's church in Norwich. We know very little about her, except that in May 1373, at the age of thirty, in the context of an acute illness from which she expected to die, she had a series of visions, which she refers to in her writing as 'revelations' or 'showings'. She subsequently wrote down her experiences, first in the form of a short account, which may have been written relatively soon after the experience, or possibly as late as 1385–8 (Mursell, 2001, p. 218), and then later, twenty years after the experience,[5] as a longer text. The long text includes additional material arising from Julian's reflections upon her experience.[6]

Julian was keen that we should not pay attention to her, but rather that her visions should direct our attention towards God:

> Everything that I say about myself I mean to apply to all my fellow Christians, for I am taught that this is what our Lord intends in this spiritual revelation. And therefore I pray you all for God's sake, and I counsel you for your own profit, that you disregard the wretched worm, the sinful creature to whom it was shown, and that mightily, wisely, lovingly and meekly you contemplate God, who out of his courteous love and his endless goodness was willing to show this vision generally, to the comfort of us all.[7]

Despite this, there has been much speculation about Julian's life. Although nothing can be known with certainty, many have suggested that she was a nun at the nearby abbey at Carrow. In contrast, Benedicta Ward (1988) has made a convincing argument that she may well have been married and widowed, possibly with at least one child of her own, and that both her husband and her child may have died in the plague. If this is true, then Julian's deep acquaintance with suffering, even prior to her own illness, becomes clear.

Julian recounts three desires that she had expressed in prayer well before her illness, the first two of which she had forgotten about by the time of the illness. All of these desires reflect a concern

---

[5]Chapter 51, p. 270.
[6]References here will all be to the translation of the long text, unless stated otherwise. The translations (of both short and long texts) by Colledge and Walsh (Colledge, Walsh and LeClercq, 1977) have been used throughout.
[7]Chapter 6 of the short text, p. 133.

to suffer, directly or indirectly, with Christ in his passion. The first desire was that she might have been with Mary Magdalene and others at the crucifixion, so that she might have seen the passion of Christ with her own eyes and suffered this experience with them. The second, which appears to have come into her mind unbidden, was that she might experience a severe illness from which it would seem that she would die. Whilst this seems a strange thing to wish for in our eyes, it is less so in a medieval Christian context and it is clear that Julian hoped it might enable her to live better thereafter for God's glory. Her third desire was to receive three metaphorical 'wounds', respectively, of true contrition, of loving compassion and of a longing for God. Brant Pelphrey (1989) speculates that these wounds might have been inspired by the story of St Cecilia, who was said to have received three wounds in the course of her martyrdom for her Christian faith.

In Chapter 2 of the long text, Julian gives a date for her visions. According to the manuscript held in the Bibliothèque Nationale in Paris (usually referred to as P) this was 13 May 1373. According to two copies of the manuscript held in the British Library in London (Sloane 1 and Sloane 2), this was 8 May. By this date, whichever date it was, Julian had been ill for five days and five nights and, being expected to die, had received the last rites two days previously. A priest who visited her brought a crucifix, upon which Julian fixed her gaze. She describes her failing sight, a darkening of the room, and a light that fell upon the cross.

> Everything around the cross was ugly and terrifying to me, as if it were occupied by a great crowd of devils.
>
> (p. 180)

Thus, the visions begin with a literal focus upon a representation of Christ's passion. The first fifteen visions that Julian experienced all appeared to her, on 8 or 13 May, between the hours of 4 am and 3 pm. During the night of that day, she awoke from a terrifying dream in which the devil appeared to her, and then experienced a sixteenth, and final, vision. Whilst the revelations were thus experienced primarily in a visual mode, they were also associated with auditory verbal experiences, or 'locutions'. Julian's own understanding of the mode of revelation of her experiences is tripartite. She identifies, and distinguishes between, 'bodily vision', 'words formed in [her] understanding', and 'spiritual vision'.[8] The last of these, spiritual vision, seems to have been at least partly ineffable and Julian is cautious about claiming to be able to fully convey the nature of this mystical experience. With regard to both the visions and words, however, she is at pains to convey accurately what she saw and heard.

Julian's illness thus occurred in the context of a pattern of devotion within which the passion of Christ was central, both objectively, as a focus of prayerful attention and meditation, and subjectively, as something with which she hoped and expected to engage in her own experiences of suffering. It is not surprising, then, that these themes were prominent in Julian's visions and locutions. In the first revelation, Julian sees blood running down from under the crown of thorns on Christ's head. In the second revelation she sees a vision of Christ's face, bloodied and discoloured. In the fourth revelation she sees Christ's body bleeding profusely, and in the eighth revelation she sees his final suffering and death. Thus, in at least four of the revelations, there is evidence of fulfilment of Julian's desire to be at the cross and to see Christ's passion by way of 'bodily vision' and to share in his suffering.

There are a variety of accounts of Julian's revelations, including one by Pelphrey in which her experiences have been systematically classified according to the mode of revelation (Pelphrey, 1989). The account offered here, in Chapter 2, will focus primarily on the locutions.

Little is known about when Julian became an anchoress. Ward (1988) speculates that this was unlikely to have happened immediately after her illness and that the short text may have been written while she was still living in her own home. Indeed, the long text may have been written there too but it would seem more likely that she became an anchoress sometime reasonably soon after writing the short text, and that the long text was written in her anchorage.

An anchoress (or anchorite) would require the support of her (or his) bishop before taking up her vocation to a solitary life.[9] Once all was agreed, and in the context of a eucharistic liturgy (quite likely a requiem mass), the anchoress would be sealed into her cell as

---

[8]Chapter 9, p. 192, and Chapter 73, p. 322.
[9]See Ramirez (2017, pp. 10–14) and Wolters (1966, pp. 21–5).

though into a tomb; there would be no door. The cell was, however, not necessarily small and a servant would have been on hand to provide supplies and remove bodily or other waste. Moreover, the anchoress could receive visitors, and may have been seen as a source of wise spiritual counsel. We know that Julian received a visit, in 1413, from Margery Kempe.

Joan of Arc

Joan of Arc[10] was born and brought up in Domrémy, now in north-eastern France and known (in her honour) as Domrémy-la-Pucelle, amidst the political turmoil and hardships of the Hundred Years' War.[11] The daughter of farmers, Jacques d'Arc and Isabellette, she was baptized at Saint-Remy and according to all accounts was a devout and popular girl who helped her parents in the fields and in the home. If anything, she seems to have been a bit too religious, being told by her friends that she was too pious and going to church when her parents thought she was working in the fields. At the age of thirteen years, she began hearing voices. We would almost certainly know little or nothing about this but for the train of events that this experience set in motion, leading eventually to a trial at which her interrogation – including her cross examination about her voices – was carefully recorded.

Joan referred to herself and was known by her contemporaries (other than the people of Domrémy) as 'La Pucelle', often translated in English as 'The Maid' or 'The Maiden'. At her trial she testified that her voices also referred to her as La Pucelle (Taylor, 2006, pp. 46–9). The word actually carries a breadth of meaning, including youth, female gender and virginity, which is not captured

---

[10]Whilst Joan will be referred to here throughout as 'Joan of Arc', as is customary in most English literature, it is acknowledged that her Christian name in French was Jeanne and that her surname is a matter of contention. Her father's surname appears to have been Darc, or d'Arc, and her mother's Romée. According to local matrilineal custom, she should have been known as Romée, but she appears to have used neither of her parent's names. For further discussion, see Tavard (1998, pp. 19–36).
[11]The brief account of Joan's life given here is based primarily on Pernoud (1964) and Nash-Marshall (1999) and also on information contained in the record of her trial (Barrett, 1931).

by any single English word. Whilst this must have been an unlikely name to adopt in a military context, for Joan it seems that it offered identification with both the virgin Mary and the saints (Margaret and Catherine) whose voices she heard.

In 1429 Joan, after various unsuccessful attempts, managed to gain an audience with the dauphin, Charles, later to become King Charles VII. There are various accounts of Joan's meeting with Charles, and she herself was resistant to speaking about this matter at her trial, but she appears to have told him that God had sent her to say that he would be crowned King in Rheims. It is reported also that Joan told him certain secrets that he believed only God could have revealed to her and this appears to have been significant in persuading him to listen to her. Following a significant theological examination of Joan in Chinon and in Poitiers in March/April, of which no detailed record now exists,[12] it was decided that she should be given permission to take action, and she was allowed to ride with the army to Orleans. After a series of battles at St Loup, Augustins and Tourelles, the siege at Orleans was lifted on 8 May. The French victory was psychologically as well as militarily important. For the English it was attributed to sorcery, and for the French it was a sign of divine favour. For both sides the story of Joan's part in it was deeply significant.

In June of 1429, Joan was involved in a further series of successful military engagements and on 17 July 1429, in no small part due to her urging, the dauphin was crowned at Rheims, just as Joan had predicted. However, in September of that year, an attack on Paris culminated in a retreat and Charles VII disbanded his army. In December he ennobled Joan and her family. On the one hand, this was a great honour for Joan, and a sign of the king's gratitude. On the other hand, it gave her responsibility for raising her own army, and distanced her from the king and his court. In March of 1430, Joan's voices warned her that she would soon be captured. In a military engagement, just outside Compiègne on 23 May 1430, Joan was cut off by the enemy, the gates of the town were closed behind her, and she was captured by the Anglo-Burgundian army.

---

[12]See Hobbins (2005, pp. 217–18), for an English translation of the 'Poitiers Conclusions', the only remaining record of the theological opinions aired at that time. This document is, however, probably best viewed as a political rather than a theological summary of what was determined (p. 240).

Initially, Joan was held prisoner by Jean de Luxembourg in relative comfort. At some point during the summer of 1430, against advice to the contrary from her voices, she tried to escape from his castle at Beaurevoir, and jumped (or fell) from the castle tower but was recaptured. In December of 1430, no ransom having been offered by Charles VII, she was handed over instead, on payment of a huge ransom reflecting her political value, to Pierre Cauchon, the Bishop of Beavais. Cauchon had her transferred to Rouen where she was held in chains in a military prison, with male guards who were in her cell with her at all times. At Rouen, between 9 January and 30 May 1431,[13] she was put on trial before an ecclesiastical court. The long list of articles of accusation against her included witchcraft, heresy and dressing in men's clothes. The proceedings culminated on 24 May in Joan's abjuration and sentencing to life imprisonment, although there appears to be some doubt as to whether she had actually had the opportunity to read the official document in which she is said to accuse herself of 'falsely pretending' about her revelations and visions.

In the final event, it was her wearing of men's clothes, rather than her voices, that was to prove more significant in determining her end. On Monday 28 May, having resumed male attire, she was deemed to have relapsed. According to one account, this was because her gaolers took away her women's clothes one night and left her only a man's clothes in which to get dressed. According to another account she resumed wearing men's clothes in order to discourage unwanted male sexual attention in an unsympathetic English prison where she was at constant risk of abuse. According to the official record she said that she resumed male attire under no compulsion, and that she never intended to take an oath not to wear men's clothes. She also reports, in the official record, that following her abjuration, St Catherine and St Margaret accused her of treason and told her 'that she had damned herself in order to save her life' (Barrett, 1931, p. 319).

Whatever the truth of the matter, Joan was deemed in a final sentence on Wednesday 30 May 1431 to be a relapsed heretic and

---

[13]Actually, a series of three trials: a preparatory trial from 9 January to 26 March clarified the charges, the main trial (ending in Joan's abjuration) from 26 March to 24 May and then a trial following her alleged relapse, from 28 to 29 May.

was sentenced to death. On the same day she was burned at the stake. Eyewitness accounts of her end are deeply moving:

> Being in the flames she ceased not until the end to proclaim and confess aloud the holy name of Jesus, imploring and invoking without cease the help of the saints in paradise.
>
> (Pernoud, 1964, p. 232)

One clergyman was recorded as saying 'I would that my soul were where I believe this woman's soul to be' (Pernoud, 1964, p. 232).

Inquests into the original trial findings were held in 1450 and 1452. At a trial of rehabilitation, beginning in 1455 a few years after the French had retaken Rouen and thus gained access to the records of the earlier trial, all the earlier charges were refuted. On 7 July 1456, the Archbishop of Rheims pronounced the earlier trial a fraud and in error and annulled its findings against Joan. Joan was pronounced innocent.

It was not until the nineteenth century that the case for Joan's canonization was seriously considered and only in 1920 that she was finally canonized. Even then, the process was marked by political concerns of the time, and by evidence of her loyalty to the church, more than by accounts of her saintliness in life (Warner, 2013, pp. 246–7).

Mental illness in the Middle Ages

What we might call today mental illness was referred to in a variety of ways in medieval literature, including – but not only – 'madness' and 'insanity' (Craig, 2014). For example, in reference to Margery Kempe's puerperal illness her *Book* says that she 'lost her reason for a long time' (p. 33) and that she 'went out of her mind' (p. 41). By whatever terminology, medieval writers recognized a group of conditions, such as phrenesis, mania and melancholia, which broadly correspond to our category of mental disorders. The causes of such conditions might include imbalance of the four bodily humours (blood, yellow bile, black bile and phlegm), demon possession or perhaps (but less certainly) divine punishment for sin, and these various factors were not necessarily mutually exclusive (Doob, 1974; Trenery and Horden, 2017).

During the period in which we are interested in this book, two kings, Charles VI of France and Henry VI of England, were afflicted by episodes of mental illness. Charles and Henry were related, and quite possibly both afflicted by an inherited disorder, variegate intermittent porphyria, which may be associated with episodes of depression and/or psychosis (Hurst, 1982), although it has also been argued that Henry may have suffered from schizophrenia (Bark, 2002). Of course, nothing was known about schizophrenia or the porphyrias in the Middle Ages, and a variety of explanations were put forward to explain the illnesses of these kings. Writing about Charles VI, Penelope Doob (1974) says:

> Charles's case is highly representative of medieval attitudes towards madness. Almost every conceivable cause is considered except for possession ....
>
> (p. 48)

The causes to which Charles' madness were variously attributed included stress, overwork, constitution, climate, poisoning, witchcraft and divine punishment, with more generous explanations being offered by friends and more blameworthy accounts provided by enemies (Doob, 1974, pp. 45–9). In contrast, the immediate cause of Henry's illness was said to be simply 'fright', although the exact nature of this fright is nowhere explained (Clarke, 1975, p. 177). The religious nature of his delusions and hallucinations, combined with his excessive piety, was such that, although he was generally considered a weak king, his episodes of illness also conveyed an air of sanctity and, after his death, his tomb became a place of pilgrimage and he was seriously considered as a candidate for canonization (Bark, 2002).

Nor was the church exempt from mental illness. The behaviour of Pope Urban VI, which led in large measure to the great schism, has variously been described as either deeply uncharitable or as evidence of mental illness. Interestingly, and even though he appears to have been one of the most controversial popes in history, much less medical attention has been devoted to diagnosing his condition than is the case with other key figures of the time, such as Charles VI and Henry VI.

Psychiatry and pathography

Pathography has been variously defined. One of Joan of Arc's pathographers has described it as 'the biographical study of eminent people, taking into account their mental and physical health' (Kenyon, 1973). Even with purely biological pathology, there are significant problems with making retrospective diagnoses for historical figures (Mitchell, 2011). The particular form of pathography with which we are concerned here is psychopathography, in which retrospective psychiatric diagnoses are made, based upon historical sources. In this context, the diagnosis becomes an explanation for unusual or remarkable behaviour and experiences (Jutel and Russell, 2021). As Jutel and Russell explain, in relation to Joan of Arc:

> Joan of Arc heard voices, dressed as a man and joined an army. She understood her experience of hearing voices as religious visions; a divine decree to diverge. She was eventually canonised in 1909. Yet, a divine explanation (the 'master narrative' of the time) holds little traction today, and in her psychopathography ... the religious explanation is replaced by a diagnostic one.
>
> (Jutel and Russell, 2021, pp. 6–7)

As these authors go on to argue later in their paper, such diagnoses tell us more about those who make the diagnosis than they do about the one diagnosed. We live in a highly medicalized society and medical categories have replace religious visions as the readily available explanations of our day. In doing this they help us to make sense of human behaviour and provide reassurance that we know what the problem is with our flawed humanity, but they do so at a great cost. They find meaning only in superficial explanations and not in any deeper existential meaning. Indeed, they render such deeper interpretations of experience and behaviour as more or less meaningless.

There is a further problem with psychopathography in that it must rely for its evidence largely upon documentary sources which were compiled and preserved for completely different purposes, and in a different age, by authors who were not looking for the signs and symptoms that we consider important in support of medical diagnosis. We therefore have no direct access to the evidence upon which a modern psychiatrist would rely for making a diagnosis.

Yet a further problem with psychopathography is that it relies upon the psychological and psychiatric understandings of the day, and these are subject to change. This is particularly important with respect to the focus of this book on experiences of hearing voices (auditory verbal hallucinations). Whereas, until relatively recently, such experiences were taken as more or less pathognomonic of psychiatric disorder, research has now shown that they are commonly experienced in the general population in the absence of any diagnosable condition. The phenomenology of such experiences – whilst different in some ways – also shows significant overlap between 'normal' and clinical groups (Cook, 2018, pp. 7–8).

In the research literature on contemporary experience, we are now more aware than ever that voice hearing may be deeply meaningful, at least in an individual and biographical sense, but also – at least sometimes – more widely (Cook, 2018). A category of spiritually significant voices has been proposed as a means of attempting to better delineate and classify such experiences (Cook et al., 2022). However, it is also becoming clear that a diagnostic approach which seeks to separate spiritual experiences from pathological ones is in itself flawed. People may have a diagnosed illness, such as bipolar disorder, and also have spiritually meaningful experiences in the context of that illness (Ouwehand et al., 2018). The questions of psychiatric diagnosis (whether or not there is evidence of illness) and spiritual discernment (whether or not an experience is spiritually meaningful) are (or should be) thus independent of each other. An experience such as the hearing of a spiritually significant voice may be a part of the constellation of symptoms of illness *and* be spiritually meaningful. On the other hand, it may be neither evidence of illness nor spiritually meaningful, or it might be evidence of one and not the other.

Spirituality in the Middle Ages

The Christian spirituality of medieval Europe was marked by both uniformity and diversity, inclusivity and intolerance, political engagement and devotional interiority. It was patriarchal in its institutional hierarchies but also selectively inclusive of female leadership and mystical experience.[14] Amidst these tensions and contradictions, it would be easy to overgeneralize and the period of the late Middle Ages with which we are concerned in this book was marked by its own particular spiritual concerns and emphases.

Ulrike Wiethaus (2005) has suggested that the western Christian spirituality of the thirteenth through to the fifteenth centuries was characterized by 'widening rifts and radical responses'. The rifts included religious divisions (antisemitism) and those between the laity and academic theologians. Radical responses, in the early thirteenth century, included the apophatic spirituality of Meister Eckhart through to Franciscan criticisms of papal authority. The *devotio moderna* movement, primarily from the low countries but exerting its influence across Germany, France and Italy, from the late fourteenth century through the end of the fifteenth century, brought together laity and clergy, in pursuit of inner holiness, meditation and virtuous living. The literature of the movement, in the vernacular, found its peak in Thomas à Kempis' *Imitation of Christ*.

Devotional practices of the late Middle Ages emphasized – amongst other things – prayer, penitence (including going to confession), pilgrimage, fasting, almsgiving, veneration of holy objects (relics, crucifixes, etc.) and the preaching and hearing of sermons. The major themes of devotion included the passion of Christ, the blessed virgin Mary, and the cult of the saints (Kieckhefer, 1988). All of these practices were later to become controversial in the European reformation. They were made visible in art, architecture, liturgy, literature, ritual and processions.

Spiritual voices and visions in historical context: lessons for psychiatry

The aim of this book is to consider the lessons for psychiatry that may emerge from a study of spiritual voices and visions in historical context, based on three medieval women: Margery Kempe, Julian

---

[14]For helpful reviews of European medieval spirituality, see Wiethaus (2005) and Raitt, McGinn and Meyendorff (1988).

of Norwich and Joan of Arc. In particular, the concern here will be with the meaningfulness of these experiences for the three women themselves, their wider world and our world today. The hope is that the diachronic perspective, across six centuries, may shed some light on contemporary issues which are less than obvious because we are over-familiar with them and too caught up in our own, peculiarly twenty-first century, ways of viewing things. However, the complexity of the task must be acknowledged at the outset requiring as it does critical attention to the historical context, the source documents, the historical-medical perspective, psychiatric phenomenology, diagnosis, theology and spirituality. In order to attend to all of this, insofar as it is possible to do so at all in a work of this length, the book will proceed along the following lines.

Chapter 1 will focus on Margery Kempe, attending first to her voice hearing and visionary experiences, as recorded in her *Book*; then, secondly, considering her illness(es) and the associated secondary diagnostic literature and then, thirdly and finally, concluding with a study of her spirituality. Chapters 2 and 3 will follow a broadly similar pattern in relation to Julian of Norwich and Joan of Arc, respectively. In Chapter 4, consideration will be given to what may be learned from these three women that may be of benefit to psychiatry today. In particular, it will be proposed that we may find meaning in experiences which are too often pathologized, and that this meaning is beneficial to patients and thus something that clinicians need to attend to much more closely. However, it will also be acknowledged that our perspectives upon such experiences reflect a deep entanglement of disciplinary and professional viewpoints and that we need to become much better – in research and in clinical practice – at a creative and critical approach to boundary crossing, which enables new therapeutic possibilities to emerge for the benefit of patients. In the Conclusion we will consider, briefly and tentatively, what a more meaningful psychiatry might look like in the light of the preceding chapters.

1

Margery Kempe

Margery's *Book*, since its rediscovery almost ninety years ago, has attracted interest from scholars from diverse disciplines and interests.[1] The first autobiography in English, it presents an account of Margery's inner world of thoughts, feelings, sexual desire and spirituality. It relates her unconventional role as a 'wandering wife' and her propensity to burst into tears in public places (Bremner, 1992). The focus here will not be on this wider, and now vast, secondary literature, but on what the *Book* tells us about the interconnections between Margery's unusual perception-like experiences and their relationships to psychiatric diagnoses and spirituality. In her *Book*, Margery describes countless religious experiences, including both visions and voices, all of which are presented as evidence for her sanctity. The *Book* also describes a number of illnesses, notably the mental illness associated with childbirth, described at the very beginning of the *Book*, and a physical illness lasting eight years, which began *c.* 1418 (described in Chapter 56 of her *Book*). The focus of this chapter will be on the relationship between Margery's recorded experiences, particularly the voices that she hears, her illness and her spirituality. First, let us consider in more detail the nature of the voices that Margery hears.

---

[1]See, for example, McEntire (1992b), Kalas (2020) and Bale (2021).

Margery's voices

Like St Bridget of Sweden, with whose life and *Revelations* Margery was acquainted, and upon whose life she quite possibly modelled her own, Margery received her divine communications both through voices and through visions (Cleve, 1992). Whilst it is her converse with heavenly and saintly voices that predominate in the *Book* as a whole, the story begins with demonic voices and with an account of voices associated with mental illness.

In Chapter 1 of her *Book*, Margery refers to an unconfessed sin about which she was often troubled:

> For she was continually hindered by her enemy – the devil – always saying to her while she was in good health that she didn't need to confess but do penance by herself alone, and all should be forgiven, for God is merciful enough ...

> And when she was at any time sick or troubled, the devil said in her mind that she should be damned, for she was not shriven of that fault.
>
> (p. 41)[2]

After the birth of her first child, Margery seeks to confess her sin, but the priest is insensitive and she feels unable to complete her confession.

> And soon after, because of the dread she had of damnation on the one hand, and his sharp reproving of her on the other, this creature went out of her mind and was amazingly disturbed and tormented with spirits for half a year, eight weeks and odd days.

> And in this time she saw, as she thought, devils opening their mouths all alight with burning flames of fire, as if they would have swallowed her in, sometimes pawing at her, sometimes threatening her, sometimes pulling her and hauling her about

---

[2]All quotations from *The Book of Margery Kempe*, and page references to *The Book*, are from Windeatt (1994). These are, of course, translations from the original Middle English text.

both night and day during the said time. And also the devils called out to her with great threats, and bade her that she should forsake her Christian faith and belief, and deny her God, his mother, and all the saints in heaven, her good works and all good virtues, her father, her mother, and all her friends. And so she did.

(p. 41)

This illness, with its visions and voices of devils, provided the context for a visionary experience in which she says that she saw Christ sit on her bedside and heard him say: 'Daughter, why have you forsaken me, and I never forsook you?' (p. 42). Following this experience she became calm and made a complete recovery. Despite this, Margery describes continuing sins of pride, envy, vanity and covetousness. The significant turning point, in terms of the change in Margery's way of life, is related at the beginning of Chapter 3 of her *Book*, when Margery is in bed with her husband one night:

she heard a melodious sound so sweet and delectable that she thought she had been in paradise ... This melody was so sweet that it surpassed all the melody that might be heard in this world, without any comparison, and it caused this creature when she afterwards heard any mirth or melody to shed very plentiful and abundant tears of high devotion, with great sobbings and sighings for the bliss of heaven ...

(p. 46)

Following this, Margery frequently speaks of the bliss of heaven, to the point of annoying people, and she loses the desire to have sexual intercourse with her husband. Her frequent weeping is also the cause of offence to others, who call her a hypocrite. She adopts penitential practices, including the wearing of a hair-cloth shirt, fasting, frequent confession, depriving herself of sleep and spending long hours in church. She also describes a period of two years when 'she had great quiet of spirit from any temptations'. However, she becomes proud and then experiences a period of three years of great temptations including, notably, the desire to commit adultery with a man to whom she is attracted.

The story takes another significant turn at the beginning of Chapter 5. As she is kneeling in church weeping and asking forgiveness for her sins:

our merciful Lord Christ Jesus – blessed may he be – ravished her spirit and said to her, 'Daughter, why are you weeping so sorely? I have come to you, Jesus Christ, who died on the cross suffering bitter pains and passion for you. I, the same God, forgive you your sins to the uttermost point. And you shall never come into hell nor into purgatory, but when you pass out of this world, with the twinkling of an eye, you shall have the bliss of heaven, for I am the same God who has brought your sins to your mind and caused you to be shriven of them. And I grant you contrition until your life's end.'

(p. 51)

This locution continues at some length, telling her that she is to address Jesus as 'Jesus, my love', and that she is to stop wearing a hair shirt, and to stop using her rosary so much, but also to stop eating meat (which she loves). She is warned that she will have enemies, but also that God will give her victory over them and will not forsake her. In place of using her rosary, she is to engage in contemplative prayer, and she is told to go and tell what she has heard to a certain anchorite attached to a local Dominican friary. When she speaks to the anchorite, he affirms the revelations that she has received and tells her that when God gives her 'such thoughts' she is to tell him about them and he will tell her whether they are from the Holy Spirit or from the devil.

From this point on, conversational exchanges between Margery and Jesus are frequent and commonplace. Thus, in Chapter 6, after she has been seeking to spend time in meditation but does not know what to think of, she says:

Jesus, what shall I think about?

Our Lord Jesus answered in her mind, 'Daughter, think of my mother, for she is the cause of all the grace that you have'.

And then at once she saw St Anne, great with child, and then she prayed St Anne to let her be her maid and her servant. And presently our Lady was born, and then she busied herself to take the child to herself and look after her until she was twelve years of age, with good food and drink, with fair white clothing and white kerchiefs. And then she said to the blessed child, 'My Lady, you shall be the mother of God.'

The blessed child answered and said, 'I wish I were worthy to be the handmaiden of her that should conceive the Son of God.'

The creature said, 'I pray you, my lady, if that grace befall you, do not discontinue with my service.'

The blessed child went away for a certain time – the creature remaining still in contemplation – and afterwards came back again and said, 'Daughter, now I have become the mother of God.'

And then the creature fell down on her knees with great reverence and great weeping and said, 'I am not worthy, my lady, to do you service.'

'Yes daughter', she said, 'follow me – I am well pleased with your service.'

(pp. 52–3)

The story continues with Margery accompanying Mary on her visit to Elizabeth and then being present at the birth of Jesus and being able to hold the infant Jesus. Margery is present when the three kings visit, and then accompanies the holy family as they flee to Egypt.

This early account, as well as later accounts of Margery's meditation on the passion of Christ, follows a pattern which might be understood as one of imaginative prayer within which the voices of Jesus, Mary and other saints might be taken as simply a part of a reflective spiritual exercise. However, the voices that Margery hears do not always fall within such an explicitly meditative framework. More often they are woven into the fabric of daily life, taking the form of conversational exchanges concerning the events and challenges of the day. Usually, such exchanges provide Margery with reassurance and affirmation. Thus, for example, when she is criticized by a priest for wearing white clothes, and is told that she has a devil, she is reassured by God that he has 'no liking' for this man (p. 121). When, on one of her journeys, she is warned that there are many thieves in the area along the way home, she is reassured by Jesus:

Don't be afraid, daughter, for you and everybody in your company shall go as safe as if they were in St Peter's church.

(p. 137)

On two occasions, when she is ill and fearing that she might die, she is reassured by Jesus that she will not die (pp. 142, 176). When two men are put in prison on her account, she is reassured that they will be released (p. 151). When she is missing the company of an anchorite who has been a source of comfort to her, she is told that someone else will come 'from far away' who will fulfil her desire (p. 181). When people are speaking badly of her, she is reassured that she has 'the true way to heaven' (p. 195). When she asks Jesus how she might best love him, he replies that:

> If you knew how sweet your love is to me, you would never do anything else but love me with all your heart.
>
> (p. 196)

When a priest is sick for whom she cares, and with whom she had hoped to speak again, she is reassured that he will not die (p. 209). Similarly, she is reassured that her husband will not die following an accident (p. 220) and that a burgess will not die from his illness (p. 243). She is reassured that her son will have a safe journey (p. 268). When she is afraid for her own safety and that of her companions in a storm at sea, she is comforted (p. 274); and in a hostile country, she is told that neither she nor her companions will be harmed (p. 277). She is given divine permission to make a journey that she has been told by her confessor she should not make (pp. 271–2).

These experiences of reassurance are often conversational exchanges, with the responding voice speaking relatively briefly, and in one place Mary (the mother of Jesus) is said to have 'chatted' with Margery (p. 85). However, there are longer discourses, as in Chapter 84. Here, Margery is told at some length, over a three-page monologue, that God knows every thought of her heart, that she will be rewarded in heaven, that God is pleased with her charity and with her prayers, that she should know that all her goodness comes from God and that she should rejoice (pp. 244–7). Similarly, in Chapter 86, there is a monologue over more than four pages (pp. 250–5) and in Chapter 88 an affirmation of Margery for the writing of her book leads into a lengthy discourse concerning her confessors.

Whilst the voices that Margery hears are usually reassuring and encouraging, she is also told by Jesus that she should expect 'much tribulation', and is 'depressed and dismayed at this' (p. 157). She is woken by a loud voice calling her name, and is frightened (p. 169). She is told to give up her fasting, even though she would have preferred to continue it, and is afraid that people will criticize her for doing so (pp. 200–1). When she prays that her tears might be taken away from her, her request is denied (p. 222). Margery is also told by God to give away all her money, including money that she has borrowed (pp. 128–9). When she wants to go out to visit some churches in Rome, she is warned not to go out, because God will send 'great storms' (p. 132). She is in great distress and doubt when she is told to leave Germany, even though she has been received warmly by the people of that country (p. 275). As described above, in Chapter 1 of her *Book* Margery is also distressed by hearing the voices of the devil and demons. Demonic voices largely disappear thereafter, although in Chapter 59 they reappear briefly.

Both divine and demonic voices are aware of Margery's thoughts, as in Chapter 1, where the devil is aware of Margery's unconfessed sin, and in certain instances where it is clear that Margery's thoughts are being answered by a voice, rather than anything that she has said out loud (pp. 269, 270–1, 275). The content of the voices also includes material that is represented as supernatural knowledge. Thus, Margery has revelations about whether or not people will die, and whether they are in purgatory (pp. 88–9), about people's honesty (pp. 91–2), about what the outcome of a local church dispute will be (pp. 94–6), about coming storms (p. 132), about whether people are going to heaven or hell (p. 183) and that there will soon be a new Prior of Lynn (p. 211).

Most commonly it is 'our Lord', or 'our Lord Jesus Christ', whose voice Margery reports hearing. In Chapter 35, where she reports being taken by God the Father as his wedded wife, she is addressed separately by both God the Father and by God the Son, and also reports third person discourse between these two persons of the Trinity. She does not appear to hold discourse with the third person of the Trinity, but rather, in Chapter 36, she reports hearing

as if it were a pair of bellows blowing in her ear ... the sound of the Holy Ghost. And then our Lord turned that sound into the voice of a dove, and afterwards he turned it into the voice of a little bird which is called a redbreast, that often sang very merrily in her right ear ... She had been used to such tokens for about twenty-five years at the time of writing this book.

(p. 127)

Margery is also addressed by a variety of saints:

Sometimes our Lady spoke to her mind; sometimes St Peter, sometimes St Paul, sometimes St Katherine, or whatever saint in heaven she was devoted to, appeared to her soul and taught her how she should love our Lord and how she should please him. These conversations were so sweet, so holy and so devout, that often this creature could not bear it, but fell down and twisted and wrenched her body about, and made remarkable faces and gestures, with vehement sobbings and great abundance of tears, sometimes saying 'Jesus, mercy', and sometimes 'I die'.

(p. 75)

Elsewhere, she reports hearing St John, St Mary Magdalene and 'many others' (p. 104); St Jerome (p. 136) and St Margaret (p. 256); and she reports on one occasion that St John heard her confession (p. 117). As in the case of her conversation with the first two persons of the Trinity, these discourses also include some third-person speech, as in Chapter 21 where, during the course of a conversation between Margery and Jesus, Jesus addresses his mother and says 'Blessed Mother, tell my daughter of the greatness of love I have for her' (p. 85).

Margery hears various non-verbal sounds in the absence of any objective external source, as in the case of the sound of the Holy Ghost (see above). She also hears music:

Sometimes she heard with her bodily ears such sounds and melodies that she could not hear what anyone said to her at that time unless he spoke louder. These sounds and melodies she had heard nearly every day for twenty-five years when this book was written, and especially when she was in devout prayer ...

(p. 124; cf p. 46)

Margery's experiences include visions as well as auditory perceptions, as in the illness reported in Chapter 1 where she sees devils. Most often these visual experiences are in the context of meditation on the gospel narratives, as in the example from Chapter 6, above, where she sees the birth of Jesus, in Chapter 82 where she sees Christ presented as a baby in the temple in Jerusalem, and elsewhere in her meditations on the passion of Christ (e.g., Chapters 57, 78–81) and the resurrection (Chapter 81). However, she also experiences more ambiguous visual phenomena, which are interpreted for her by 'our Lord':

> She saw with her bodily eyes many white things flying all about her on all sides, as thickly in a way as specks in a sunbeam; they were very delicate and comforting, and the brighter the sun shone, the better she could see them. She saw them at many different times and in many different places ... And many times she was afraid what they might be, for she saw them at night in darkness as well as in daylight. Then when she was afraid of them, our Lord said to her, 'By this token, daughter, believe it is God who speaks in you, for wherever God is, heaven is, and where God is, there are many angels, and God is in you and you are in him. And therefore, don't be afraid, daughter, for these betoken that you have many angels around you, to keep you both day and night so that no devil shall have power over you, nor evil men harm you.'

> (p. 124)

Margery also reports perceptions in the olfactory modality:

> Sometimes she sensed sweet smells in her nose; they were sweeter, she thought, than any earthly sweet thing ever was that she smelled before, nor could she ever tell how sweet they were, for she thought she might have lived on them had they lasted.

> (p. 124)

And, finally, Margery reports a bodily experience of heat:

> Our Lord also gave her another token which lasted about sixteen years, and increased ever more and more, and that was a flame of fire of love – marvellously hot and delectable and very comforting, never diminishing but ever increasing; for though the weather were never so cold she felt the heat burning in her breast and at her heart, as veritably as a man would feel the material fire if he put his hand or his finger into it.

> (pp. 124–5)

Whilst Margery's experiences are clearly identifiable according to perceptual modalities of hearing, sight, smell, etc., it is not always clear whether she is reporting a literal perceptual experience, or something more imaginative or metaphorical. Where she reports music so loud that people have to speak up in order that she might hear them, we may perhaps infer that this is a literally perceptual (if hallucinatory) experience. However, elsewhere, she explicitly contrasts what she has heard with bodily sensory experience:

> Then our Lord sent St John the Evangelist to hear her confession, and she said 'Benedicite' and he said 'Dominus' truly in her soul, so that she saw him and heard him in her spiritual understanding as she would have done another priest by her bodily sense.
>
> (p. 117)

In many other places, she reports that she was 'answered in her mind' (p. 52), that 'our Lord said in her mind' (p. 65), 'I am commanded in my soul' (p. 69), 'she was commanded in her spirit' (p. 80), 'our Lord Jesus Christ spoke to her in her soul' (p. 176), 'she saw in her soul' (p. 214), 'our Lord spoke … saying to her spiritual understanding' (p. 251), 'she was answered in her thought' (p. 271), she hears 'Our merciful Lord, speaking in her mind' (p. 274) and so-on. The sheer number of such references suggests that Margery is most often reporting either an imaginative experience, or else something that is at least perceived within her own thoughts, and not in external space.

Margery's illness

Margery's illness has proved to be no less controversial than her reported visions and voices. It is notable that the *Book* opens with an account of the great bodily sickness, through which she lost her reason for a long time (p. 33).

As described above, this illness arose following the birth of her first child and came to an end, at least in her own understanding, with a vision of Christ. The course of the illness, over more than six months, was marked by experiences 'as she thought' of devils which threatened and called out to her, bidding her to forsake her Christian faith and kill herself. This episode is thus identified by Margery herself as having significant physical (bodily), mental and spiritual dimensions. For modern commentators, it is usually identified as being a puerperal psychosis – that is, a major mental illness arising during the post-natal period – characterized by visual, auditory verbal and somatic hallucinations. However, given that Margery reports a full recovery from this illness, the question arises as to how her subsequent visions and voices should be explained, not to mention her weeping, her constant preoccupation with religious themes and other aspects of her conversation and behaviour.

Following the discovery of the full manuscript of Margery's *Book* in 1934, there was much reference to Margery as suffering from hysteria. Thus, in 1936, Herbert Thurston (1936) writes

That Margery was a victim of hysteria can hardly be open to doubt, for apart from her weeping fits, she was constantly subject to mysterious illnesses from which she suddenly recovered.

(p. 452)

Later he writes that Margery was

a neurotic and self-deluded visionary who had nothing about her of the spirit of God. The problem which confronts us in case after case of these queer mystics is the combination of pronounced hysteria with a genuine love of God, great generosity and self-sacrifice, unflinching courage, and very often the occurrence of strange psychic phenomena, particularly in the form of a knowledge of distant and future events.

(p. 455)

Many subsequent authors have agreed with this diagnosis. Thus, Trudy Drucker (1972) considered that

What evolved in Margery's case was a full-blown and apparently lifetime but episodic case of hysteria that was to take particularly bizarre forms.

(p. 2911)

In addition to acknowledging that she also experienced a postpartum psychosis, Drucker additionally diagnoses episodes of falling due to epilepsy and visual phenomena due to migraine. Drucker thus resorts eventually to no less than four diagnoses in order to explain Margery's symptoms across the course of her lifetime.

Richard Lawes (1999) rightly points out that the term 'hysteria' is not represented in more recent diagnostic systems and that historically it has been employed in negative fashion, primarily with reference to women. Rather more debatably, he concludes that Margery does not meet DSMIV criteria for histrionic personality disorder, the equivalent current category. In order to support this conclusion, he argues that Margery does not show evidence of such criteria as those concerned with attention seeking, 'rapidly shifting and shallow expression of emotions', use of physical appearance to draw attention to herself and self-dramatization, all of which might well be said to be supported by evidence in abundance in the text of Margery's *Book*.

For some, however, it is the evidence for her earlier puerperal illness that is taken as most convincing and this is extrapolated to include all her later behaviour. Thus, Claridge et al. (1990), having noted the possibility of the diagnosis of hysteria, write:

> It is more likely that she was a schizophrenic, for whom the religious beliefs of her day provided a means of escape from the daily life with which her inadequate personality could not cope.
>
> (p. 61)

Given the concurrent affective symptomatology, and identifying her later as well as earlier (postpartum) visionary experiences and voices as hallucinatory, these authors finally conclude that an appropriate diagnosis would be schizo-affective disorder (p. 69).

In similar vein, Marlys Craun (2005), writing in the journal *Psychiatric Services*, argues simply and succinctly (but, one might add, rather uncritically) that 'Kempe was psychotic for much of her adult life' (p. 655). Freeman et al. (1990) find both hysteria and postpartum psychosis to be inadequate diagnoses and identify evidence in Margery's text for

> distinct periods of illness in which episodes of mania and melancholia alternate with each other or are mixed, followed by a mystical experience wherein Jesus reorders her world.
>
> (p. 188)

Their diagnosis is thus one of bipolar disorder (p. 190).

In contrast to this, Richard Lawes (1999, pp. 153–4) argues for a diagnosis of depressive psychosis which resolves in the context of a healing mystical experience of a vision of Christ. He does not find convincing the arguments of Freeman et al. for evidence of an ongoing affective psychosis, and takes seriously Margery's own distinction between her earlier illness and her later religious experiences.

For yet other authors, whilst acknowledging the early episode of postpartum psychosis, Margery's later behaviour and experiences are interpreted not as evidence of ongoing psychosis, but rather as adaptive and insightful. Thus, Jefferies and Horsfall (2014) write that Margery

> was a remarkable woman who used her special relationship with the divine to make meaning of her episode of postnatal psychosis and to live the life that she desired.
>
> (p. 362)

In similarly sympathetic vein, Alison Torn (2008) points out that

> it is important to identify the literary roots and social and historical contexts of Kempe's book in order not to misconstrue the central religious scenes as madness.
>
> (p. 88)

And to quote just one more example, Roy Porter (1996) suggests:

> [Margery] knew that many people thought her voices and visions – indeed, her whole course of life – signified madness, to be attributed to illness or the Devil. She pondered that dilemma deeply, and sought advice. But the path to which she aspired – a closer walk, a spiritual communion, marriage even with God – was a path legitimate within the beliefs of her times …
>
> (p. 111)

William Ober (1985) also understands Margery as having made a complete recovery from her postpartum psychosis, but understands her as continuing to suffer from a form of hysteria. According to Ober, 'increased autosuggestibility' provides a common denominator for both hysteria and mystical experience and thus he is able to reconcile the two without detracting from the validity of the latter. Indeed, he sees the latter as 'a valid solution to her emotional problems in the context of her time' (p. 39).

The psychiatrist Anthony Ryle, quoted by Stephen Medcalf (1981, pp. 114–15),[3] is less sure that Margery made a complete and permanent recovery from her early psychosis, and finds evidence for diagnosing a brief recurrence, lasting a week or two, in which she was deluded and possibly also hallucinated.[4] However, he does not consider this diagnosis to be the basis of her claim to a special relationship with God, or to her 'conspicuous activities' (dressing in white, weeping, etc.), all of which he believes to be related to an 'hysterical personality organization'.

Santha Bhattacharji (1997) argues that Margery's crying, far from being evidence of hysteria, is actually to be understood within the context of a medieval spiritual tradition that was affirmative of tears. She argues that this tradition is to be found in Walter Hilton's *Ladder of Perfection* and in Richard Rolle's *Incendium Amoris*, both of which we know were read to Margery, as well as in the life of Marie d'Oignies, also referred to in Margery's *Book*. Similarly, she sees Margery's visions as fitting into a mediaeval devotional practice of meditation which would have been known to Margery at least in Bridget of Sweden's *Revelations*, if not also from other sources. Bhattacharji also finds precedent for Margery's conversations with Christ, notably in Bridget of Sweden and Catherine of Siena, but here there is a marked discrepancy between the theological nature of the discourses that Bridget and Catherine report and the personal emphasis on Margery's own journey and vocation.

Having argued against diagnoses of histrionic personality disorder and ongoing psychosis, Richard Lawes argues that Margery does show evidence of temporal lobe epilepsy, including olfactory, visual and auditory hallucinations, and *deja vu*. However, he also acknowledges that there is in Margery's experiences evidence of medieval iconography:

---

[3]The quotation appears to represent a personal communication with the author, and as far as I have been able to ascertain there is no other primary source publication on Margery Kempe by Dr Ryle.
[4]This presumably refers to the episode in Chapter 59.

In this awkward synthesis of a spiritual 'template' with actual experience of an illness we see both the clumsiness of expression and the high and ardent spiritual aspiration which so often colour the *Book's* portrait of Margery Kempe.

(p. 167)

We thus find in the secondary literature a bewildering variety of medical opinion, ranging from psychosis to hysteria, from the sympathetic to the highly unsympathetic, from one diagnosis to several. Amongst the more unsympathetic opinion there is a disconcerting trend towards reductionism; but even if this pitfall is avoided, Margery's account of her life remains controversial. Viewed by some as giving evidence of a creative and adaptive form of mysticism, and by others as attention seeking and lacking in humility, it is amenable to diverse interpretations and evaluations. Few would argue that it provides revelations of universal or enduring value in the way that Julian's book does, but equally its individuality, its engagement with the realities of difficult human relationships and differences of opinion, its struggles with everyday virtue and vice, its evidence of human kindness, courage and generosity, and its obvious honesty and genuineness all lend colour, interest and attractiveness. The richness of this account is rendered the more interesting by recognizing that the realities of family life and marriage, illness and personality, and the particular historical, religious and cultural context, all make Margery's *Book* relevant to ordinary everyday human experience, and do not remove the reader to an ethereal or saintly realm. Ironically, it would seem likely that Margery did hope to present herself as a saint, but if the value of her *Book* lays more in her flawed humanity than in her sanctity, that may even be more of a tribute to her than she ever imagined.

We should note that much of the diagnostic opinion proffered in the secondary literature arises from lay authors and not from mental health professionals. Amongst the above-mentioned authors, Gordon Claridge, Phyliss Freeman and Alison Torn are psychologists; Marlys Craun is a social worker; Diana Jefferies is a nurse and only Diane Sholomskas (a co-author with Freeman) and Anthony Ryle (quoted by Medcalf) are psychiatrists. Whilst anyone may have an opinion on diagnosis, it does not appear to be only, or even primarily, the world of psychiatry that is keen to diagnose Margery. A diagnosis may provide hermeneutical justification for not taking Margery seriously, it may provide a basis for a subtle literary form of epistemic injustice and it may be consciously or unconsciously used as a way of tarnishing Margery's reputation as an author. Diagnosis may be used more widely as a means of scientific reductionism, within which theological meaning is denied. In this way, it is not only Margery whose life is denied meaning. A whole range of saints and mystics, not to mention ordinary religious people and patients in current day psychiatric clinics, are hermeneutically disenfranchised. On this view of things, Margery's experiences become meaningless – but so do the experiences of all religious people.

Margery's spirituality

How may we evaluate the relevance and meaning of Margery's *Book* today? Much of the response to the *Book* after its rediscovery in the twentieth century was negative, and much of this negativity was associated with gender stereotypes of the 'hysterical' woman, within which there also lay some equally disconcerting prejudices towards mental illness. More recently, it has become fashionable to assess Margery's *Book* more positively, a fashion which has tended to play down evidence for mental illness (except perhaps the earlier, puerperal, illness) and which has generally been inattentive to Margery's voices. All of this may make it quite difficult to achieve any degree of objectivity in discerning the enduring value of the *Book*, but an attempt must at least be made.

Hope Allen (Meech and Allen, 1940) famously, or perhaps notoriously, referred to Margery as a 'minor mystic' (p. lxi). In the preface to the first published text of Margery's *Book* after its rediscovery, she wrote that

> Margery as revealed by herself in her reminiscences ... was petty, neurotic, vain, illiterate, physically and nervously over-strained; devout, much-travelled, forceful and talented.
>
> (p. lxiv)

However, she also commented on Margery's honesty, originality and creativity. She further found significant value in the *Book*:

I do not believe that Margery's book can be explained, as I first thought, as merely the naïve outburst of an illiterate woman, who had persuaded two pliant men to write down her egotistical reminiscences.

(p. lvii)

Neither did she see Thurston's early publications on Margery's alleged hysteria as a reason to dismiss Margery. Rather, taking on board this diagnosis, she saw Margery's suggestibility as an historical resource, by means of which Margery, in giving account of her responses to the opposition that she encountered, reflected back the spiritual ideals of her day, even if she herself could not take them on board.

In a much more positive assessment of Margery, Sandra McEntire (1992a), drawing on the work of Carol Christ (1980) on feminine spirituality, identifies a pattern of self-negation, followed by awakening to new spiritual possibilities of affirming a feminine spirituality in which childbearing, midwifery, affirmation of 'spiritual virginity' and spiritual marriage all find a place. In this way her identity is both transformed and affirmed. It is interesting to reflect on the part that voices play in this process. It is demonic voices that are involved in the self-negation that is a part of her early puerperal illness. Self-awakening begins with the appearance of Christ, and his words spoken to her, at the end of this illness. The affirmation of her new identity is heard in Christ's words affirming her spiritual virginity, and at her spiritual 'marriage' to him.

Santha Bhattacharji (1997) identifies a series of 'charges' levelled against Margery under three main headings. First is that her mystical experiences are actually the result of mental illness; the second that by claiming to be a mystic she engineers for herself a more exciting life, more attention and greater status than she might otherwise have had; and the third that her experiences are self-indulgent and contain little of value to others. Bhattacharji defends Margery against each of these charges in turn. The mental illness she sees as confined to the early puerperal illness. The later allegedly 'hysterical' and attention-seeking behaviour she sees as having its precedent in the writings and behaviour of other medieval mystics, and thus not unusual. The visions she sees as in keeping with a medieval tradition of meditation on the life of Christ, thus also not unusual, and as charting the steps of Margery's spiritual growth. Her conversations, with Christ and Mary and other saints, similarly, are not without precedent. More importantly, she finds these dialogues expressive of a distinctive spirituality and teaching which have their own peculiar value.

Bhattacharji sees in Margery a mysticism that is concerned with everyday life, and in which she expresses true contrition for her own sins and seeks the repentance and forgiveness of others. She seeks, and to some extent experiences, her own union with God in a way not completely dissimilar from other mystics of the time. Over and against the 'difficult personality' that pervades much of Book I, Bhattacharji notes that Margery later spends much time quietly in King's Lynn, that she nurses her husband during his final illness, devotes much time to prayer and values relationships. Much of the apparent preoccupation with self is actually a reflection of her deep insecurity.

In his authoritative overview of *English Spirituality*, Gordon Mursell (2001), having noted that Margery evokes perhaps more 'sharply divergent reactions' than any other English spiritual author, goes on to propose that Margery was a lay woman engaged in a spiritual quest. He notes, as have other authors, that Margery has much in common with other mystics of the time all of whom have received a more positive assessment, including a commitment to chastity in the context of marriage, the pursuit of pilgrimage, devotion to the sufferings of Christ and experiences of being criticized and misunderstood. Even the tears, which clearly attracted so much negative attention during Margery's lifetime, and have continued to be a focus of controversy since, have their precedents. As much as many other saints and mystics, Margery shows herself devoted to seeking God, but she does this amidst the rather unromantic context of mental illness, failed business ventures, marital commitment and human irritability, jealousy and hostility.

Mursell also finds in Margery's book an emphasis on finding God within. Amongst the examples that he quotes in support of this finding Margery's voices (and also her affirming encounter with Julian of Norwich) play a significant part. Thus, for example, Christ says to Margery in Book I, Chapter 77:

> You also well know, daughter, that I sometimes send many great rains and sharp showers, and sometimes only small and gentle

drops. And just so I proceed with you, daughter, when it please me to speak in your soul.

(Windeatt, 1994, p. 223)

If Mursell is correct in asserting this emphasis, one possible interpretation would be that Margery understood her dialogue with Christ – and thus perhaps all her voices – as a much more interior phenomenon (within her own thoughts) than is sometimes presumed to be the case. In this way, it might be more like the experience of many contemporary Christians who hear the voice of God, or who claim that 'God put a thought into my mind …' (Dein and Cook, 2015).

Notwithstanding the contemporary trend to find more of value in Margery's *Book* than was previously acknowledged, there are still significant concerns to be addressed.

David Russell (2013) refers to the way in which he believes the text of Margery's *Book* 'conceals the evidence of likely manipulation – not only from the reader but also from Margery herself' (p. 77). Thus, given her lack of status, her quest to gain authority requires first that she convince others that she is 'directly authorised by Christ', and then that she negotiate with 'increasingly higher levels of the ecclesiastical establishment' to gain recognition of her authority (p. 79). However, these negotiations do not lead her to any leadership role or participation in community activities. For Russell, the image that emerges from the text is of

> an astute, essentially self-centred, lone figure who uses her considerable political and commercial awareness to manage her own cause, and who struggles against the world and herself with the sole motive of satisfying what Christ demands of her. Her internalised debates with him through soul-to-God conversations are the channel she uses to resolve her problems and justify her plans.
>
> (p. 87)

Margery's conversations with the voices of Christ, Mary and other saints are thus very significant, consciously or unconsciously, in engineering circumstances and support:

Christ guides Margery via their frequent mystical conversations, and she claims that he helps her by setting her objectives, gathering her allies, achieving her objectives with their support, and dealing with the many tribulations and difficulties that come into her life. She is effectively, albeit supposedly unconsciously, managing Christ to create the circumstances that enable her to manage her spiritual life.

(p. 88)

Like Mursell, Russell comments on internalization as a key feature of Margery's spirituality. She often relies on her internal relationship with Christ as her sole source of authority, and even when others are drawn in as additional sources of support, it is her interior visions and conversations that are presented as reasons why they should support her.

Wolfgang Riehle (2014, p. 280), having acknowledged that his own view of Margery has changed for the better over the years, finds that Margery's life conforms with many medieval expectations of what a holy life should look like, and suggests that now only the frequency and intensity of her tears might be considered exceptionable. However, he also observes a lack of joy in Margery's book. In this respect, he finds a significant contrast with Julian, Richard Rolle and other medieval mystics. He notes the lack of hymnody, the lack of extolling of God.

Reflecting on this diverse array of assessments, it seems to me that we may identify a number of tensions in Margery's spirituality. On the one hand, Margery is very relational, conversational and engaged with her own bodily and inner (psychological) experiences, including her spiritually significant voices. Within this spirituality of relationality and engagement there is, however, a fundamental insecurity. She presents her experiences, whether intentionally or otherwise, in such a way as to generate social conflict and criticism and, at the same time, seeks reassurance from others about these same experiences. Whilst constantly seeking reassurance – whether from clergy, anchorites or others – she also appears to have had great difficulty in consciously questioning (or allowing others to question) her experiences. Her inner voices are never subjected to the kind of critique that, for example, John of the Cross might have urged her to accept concerning their potential to mislead. She does not give us examples of instances where she discerns that her voices lack divine authority. Perhaps this is an unreasonable expectation? As Riehle and others have argued, in many ways, she conforms to contemporary expectations. However, she does not engage with contemporaries who might have taken a different view. For example, whilst she is clearly familiar with 'Hilton's book', she seemingly does not take to heart his argument that 'visions or revelations by spirits, whether seen in bodily form or in the imagination ... do not constitute true contemplation' (Sherley-Price, 1988). Perhaps she does not see herself as a contemplative, and therefore imagines that these words do not apply to her? Or perhaps, consciously, or unconsciously, she excludes from her *Book* the voices that might undermine her own hagiography?

In conclusion, I suggest, we should neither move to whitewash Margery, nor pretend that her spirituality is simply the same as others of her time, for it is clearly not. Margery's spirituality is compelling for its honesty and naivete, and for her faithfulness to what she believed to be the voices of God within her. She grounds her love for Christ in her conversational familiarity with him, in her femininity and in her finding of more to life than the conventional role allotted to her in patriarchal medieval society. She is compellingly honest about her faults but finds it difficult to accept any criticism of the external displays of religiosity which are justified by her inner voices. We are left wondering about the depth of her self-awareness, insofar as she seems unable to seriously question whether her voices may not be from God. Rather, she seeks social support for their authenticity. We are left wondering about whether they draw attention to Margery rather than to God. They reassure Margery more than they reassure others about Margery. Nonetheless, they confer meaning on her life and, if we take her at her word, Margery's conscious intentions are clearly good. As she says, in the face of criticism, at the end of Chapter 3 of Book I:

all the while she thanked God for everything, desiring nothing but mercy and forgiveness of sin.

2

Julian of Norwich

Julian's *Revelations* describes a series of visions, almost all accompanied by voices, which she experienced on 8 or 13 May 1373 in the context of a life-threatening illness. In addition to the description of the immediate experience, the longer version of the text also provides the fruits of two decades of reflection on the meaning of these experiences. The basic pattern of this chapter will be similar to that followed in Chapter 1 in respect of Margery Kempe. Consideration will be given to the relationships between Julian's experiences, particularly the voices that she hears, her illness and her spirituality. However, Julian's work is very different to Margery's *Book*, particularly in terms of its theological engagement, and so the pattern will be modified slightly. First, consideration will be given to the place of locutions (voices) within the *Revelations*, then to what we know about the nature of the voices and visions that Julian experienced. Second, we will consider what is known about Julian's illness. Finally, in thinking about Julian's spirituality, will also need to give some attention to her theology as the two are inextricably intertwined.

The revelations

All but one of the revelations, at least in the long text, are associated with a locution of one kind or another.

In the **first revelation**, in addition to the bodily vision of Christ's head bleeding, Julian experiences a spiritual vision of St Mary, the mother of Christ, and also she sees something small, no bigger than a hazelnut, lying in the palm of my hand, as it seemed to me, and it was as round as a ball. I looked at it with the eye of my understanding and thought: What can this be? I was amazed that it could last, for I thought that because of its littleness it would suddenly have fallen into nothing. And I was answered in my understanding: It lasts and always will, because God loves it; and thus everything has being through the love of God.

(p. 183)[1]

We are introduced here to what I will call the 'conversational' nature of many of the locutions. Thus, in this case, the locution comes in response to a question that Julian poses in her thoughts, rather as one person might ask a question of another person and then receive an answer in response. However, it is also clear, in this example at least, that the conversation is one that takes place completely within Julian's own mind. She sees the vision with the 'eye of ... understanding', she thinks 'What can this be?' and she is answered 'in [her] understanding'. This example might easily be understood merely as the kind of internal dialogue that any person might have when thinking. Thus, we could paraphrase and might imagine a train of thought such as this:

Thought:	'What is this?'
Answering thought:	'It looks like a hazelnut, but it is SO small.'
Thought:	'How can something so small exist at all?'
Answering thought:	'It can only exist because God has created it and wants it to last.'

All of this is understandable within the range of normal human experience of thought, in contrast to the perception (bodily vision) of the bleeding from Christ's head (p. 190). The spiritual vision of the thing no bigger than a hazelnut is said by Julian to have been shown to her by Christ, and thus it has a link to the bodily vision of Christ that she has experienced. It does not itself necessarily demonstrate anything outside the range of normal human experience, albeit

---

[1] All quotations from *Revelations*, and page references to *Revelations*, are from Colledge, Walsh and LeClercq (1977). They are, of course, translations from the Middle English. They relate to the long text, unless otherwise specified.

perhaps inspired, and capable of interpretation in such a way as to render it deeply meaningful. Nonetheless, as Colledge and Walsh argue (Colledge et al., 1977, p. 29), the general thrust of Julian's account of things is that she could not find the answers within herself. It is as though they have come to her from a source outside her own mind and intellect.

In the **second revelation**, Julian wants to see the bodily vision of Christ's face more clearly, and she is answered 'in [her] reason':

> If God wishes to show you more, he will be your light; you need none but him.

(p. 193)

Whilst this answer is in Julian's reason, and thus may again be understood as her own thought, it is also here an answer to her own thought, as though from an unidentified external source. At the very least it is an answering thought in which Julian addresses herself as a second party to an internal conversation. Thus, she does not think 'If God wants to show me more, he will be my light ...', but rather she is addressed: 'If God wishes to show you more ...' The answer to her implicit request to see more clearly comes not from God but from an unidentified source. Thus, we are left free to infer either that this answer is understood by Julian as coming from an external third party (perhaps an angel), or else that it is her own thought, albeit one inspired by God.

If we were to paraphrase this train of thought, it might go something like this:

Thought:	'I wish I could see this vision more clearly.'
Answering thought:	'If God wanted you to see more clearly, you would. He is the light that enables you to see this vision at all – you need no more than this.'

Again, this train of thought has its origin in a bodily vision, and thus a highly unusual kind of perception or perception-like thought. However, the locutional thoughts in themselves are not necessarily unusual. Whilst the second thought allows the possibility of inferring external agency, it is not necessary to do so. Thus, if I'm having difficulty reading a magazine in my living room when it is getting dark, I might similarly think to myself: 'You need to turn the lights on!'

In the **third revelation**, Julian has a vision of God:

> in an instant of time, that is to say in my understanding, by which vision I saw that he is present in all things.
>
> (p. 197)

In the short text, there is no clear locution associated with this vision. However, in the long text Julian engages in a slightly longer reflection upon what she has seen. Towards the end of this, she says:

> God revealed all this most blessedly, as though to say: See, I am God. See, I am in all things. See, I do all things. See, I never remove my hands from my works, nor ever shall without end. See, I guide all things to the end that I ordain them for, before time began, with the same power and wisdom and love with which I made them; how should anything be amiss? So was the soul examined, powerfully, wisely and lovingly, in this vision.
>
> (p. 199)

While Julian attributes these words 'as though' to God, she asserts without qualification that this is a revelation from God, and she understands them as summarizing something about the way in which she experiences herself as 'examined' by God in the vision. This locution is thus clearly spoken by God, in a way that the locutions associated with the first two revelations were not. We might still understand it as Julian's own thought. That is, after twenty years of contemplating this vision, we might say, this is what Julian thought that God was saying to her through it. However, Julian's reflected view on the vision is a bit more confident, a bit less tentative, than that interpretation might allow. Even if these words were not a part of the original experience, that is not to say that Julian did not perceive them as being spoken to her by God at some later time.

In the **fourth revelation**, the bleeding of Christ's body is so copious that it seems to Julian that if it had been real, her bed would have been soaked in blood. This 'seeming' is clearly Julian's own thought, but then she says:

> it came into my mind that God has created bountiful waters on the earth for our use and our bodily comfort, out of the tender

love he has for us. But it is more pleasing to him that we accept for our total cure his blessed blood to wash us of our sins, for there is no drink that is made which it pleases him so well to give us. For it is most plentiful, as it is most precious, and that through the power of the blessed divinity. And it is of our own nature, and blessedly flows over us by the power of his precious love.

(p. 200)

Here, a thought comes into Julian's mind in response to her own reflection (her own thoughts) on the copiousness of the bleeding that she sees. Perhaps this too is her own thought, but she appears to distinguish between what 'seems' to her and what 'comes' into her thoughts. Thus, as with the 'answer' of reason in the second revelation, there is a kind of thought in Julian's mind which she identifies as being semi-autonomous, coming as though from an external source, as though (we might say) inspired.

The **fifth revelation** is a locution without a vision, to the effect that the devil is overcome by Christ's passion. At the opening of Chapter 13, as Julian is continuing to contemplate the content of the earlier revelations, she says that God:

without voice and without opening of lips, formed in my soul this saying: With this the fiend is overcome.

(p. 201)

While the qualifications, 'without voice and without opening of lips', might be taken to affirm that this voice is not 'out loud', yet she here confidently attributes the words of the locution specifically and unambiguously to God. This is a voice 'without voice', a mystical experience that defies adequate description, but the words are clearly understood by Julian as being what God has said. They are 'formed' within her mind. Rather like the thought that 'came into [Julian's] mind' in the fourth revelation, they retain some quality of being her own thoughts, albeit inspired by God.

The **sixth revelation** is also a locution:

After this our Lord said: I thank you for your service and your labour in your youth. And in this my understanding was lifted up to heaven, where I saw our Lord God as a lord in his own house ...

(p. 203)

Here the form of the locution is given no description. Perhaps we are to assume that, as in the fifth revelation, it is also 'without voice and without opening of lips'? However, it is confidently asserted as being from God, and it is clear that Julian is thoroughly convinced of its source. It leads to an imaginative vision of God in heaven, and then to a reflection on the degrees of bliss that human souls experience in heaven.

The **seventh revelation** is of alternating experiences of well-being and of woe, and has a more affective quality. Although referred to by Julian as a 'vision', it is not a vision in a bodily visual sense, and neither does it include a locution.

The **eighth revelation** includes a locution which again has an internal, conversational quality:

> Then there came a suggestion, seemingly said in friendly manner, to my reason: Look up to heaven, to his Father. And then I saw clearly by the faith which I felt that there was nothing between the cross and heaven which could have grieved me. Here I must look up or else answer. I answered inwardly with all the power of my soul, and said: No, I cannot, for you are my heaven.
>
> (p. 211)

The voice that speaks in 'friendly manner' is clearly neither God, nor Julian's own voice, and yet Julian's reply ('you are my heaven'), equally clearly, *is* addressed to God. This creates some ambiguity as to exactly whose voice this locution represents. Later, in the thirteenth revelation, she speaks of a 'friendly intermediary' who answers her in a similar way (p. 236), and who is perhaps even more clearly identified as being neither God nor Julian.

The **ninth revelation** is usually understood to commence in Chapter 22, although Colledge and Walsh (Colledge et al., 1977, p. 46) see it as beginning with Chapter 21, in which Julian's vision of the passion undertakes a transition from an affective tone of pain and grief to one of joy at what Christ's suffering has achieved. In Chapter 21, there is a further example of a locution of a 'suggested' kind:

> then cheerfully our Lord suggested to my mind: Where is there now any instant of your pain or of your grief?
>
> (p. 215)

In Chapter 22, the locutional conversation continues in a more direct manner:

> Then our good Lord put a question to me: Are you well satisfied that I suffered for you? I said: Yes, good Lord, all my thanks to you; yes, good Lord, blessed may you be. Then Jesus our good Lord said: If you are satisfied, I am satisfied. It is a joy, a bliss, an endless delight to me that I ever suffered my Passion for you; and if I could suffer more, I should suffer more. In response to this my understanding was lifted up into heaven, and there I saw three heavens ...
>
> (p. 216)

Julian describes the **tenth revelation** as being of 'how our Lord Jesus displays his heart split in two for love' (p. 176). Whilst it has something of a visual visionary content ('our good Lord looked into his side', p. 220), and again focuses on an aspect of the passion of Christ, it is actually much more locutional in form. Julian finds her understanding 'drawn' to Christ's side, the blood and water that issue from the spear wound are 'brought to mind', a part of Christ's divinity is 'showed' to her understanding, and then she continues:

> And with this our good Lord said most joyfully: See how I love you, as if he had said, my darling, behold and see your Lord, your God, who is your Creator and your endless joy; see your own brother, our saviour; my child, behold and see what delight and bliss I have in your salvation, and for my love rejoice with me.
>
> (p. 221)

Here, the locution is simply 'See how I love you' and everything that follows the words 'as if he had said' appears to be Julian's interpretation or understanding of the locution. Again, in the following paragraph, Julian says that for her 'greater understanding' the words 'See how I love you' were said, and then again she continues 'as if he had said ...' and provides still further commentary upon them. Finally, she concludes:

> This is the understanding, as simply as I can say it, of these blessed words: See how I loved you. Our Lord revealed this to make us glad and joyful.
>
> (p. 221)

Julian thus repeats the locution three times,[2] in each case following it with an attempt to convey her understanding of exactly what it meant. The reader is left with the impression that the words 'See how I loved you' were heard by Julian in a very specific way, but that her understanding of them encompassed much more than the words alone. That is, the revelation constituted not simply the words themselves, but also a mystical understanding of what was intended by them.

The **eleventh revelation** begins with a visual reference, followed by another short and specific locution, following which Julian again uses the words 'as if he had said' as a device by which to associate them with the broader mystical understanding that has been shown to her:

> And with this same appearance of mirth and joy our good Lord looked down, and brought to my mind where our Lady stood at the time of his Passion, and he said: Do you wish to see her? And these sweet words were as if he had said, I know well that you wish to see my blessed mother, for after myself she is the greatest joy that I could show you, and the greatest delight and honour to me, and she is what all my blessed creatures most desire to see.
>
> (pp. 221–2)

After further commentary by Julian, and a further expansion on an understanding of these words as addressed to all humankind, she eventually responds to them, saying:

> Yes, good Lord, great thanks, yes, good Lord, if it be your will.
>
> (p. 222)

In return, she is granted a spiritual, but not bodily, vision of Mary.

In the **twelfth revelation** Julian is granted a vision of Christ glorified, about which she says only a little, and then a much longer locution:

---

[2]In the original Middle English, in contrast to the Colledge and Walsh's translation, the tense does not change with the third repetition. In each case, the words are exactly the same: 'Lo, how that I lovid the'.

Again and again our Lord said: I am he, I am he, I am he who is highest. I am he whom you love I am he in whom you delight. I am he whom you serve. I am he for whom you long. I am he whom you desire. I am he whom you intend. I am he who is all. I am he whom Holy Church preaches and teaches to you. I am he who showed himself before to you. The number of the words surpasses my intelligence and my understanding and all my powers, for they were the most exalted, as I see it, for in them is comprehended I cannot tell what; but the joy which I saw when they were revealed surpasses all that the heart may think or the soul can desire. And therefore these words are not explained here, but let every man accept them as our Lord intended them, according to the grace God gives him in understanding and love.

(p. 223)

Thus, in contrast to the tenth and eleventh revelations, where a short locution is followed by an expansive account of Julian's understanding, here we find a locution with a number of words which surpasses Julian's understanding, and which she invites the reader to understand 'according to the grace God gives'.

The long **thirteenth revelation** opens with Julian realizing that nothing prevents her longing for God being fulfilled but sin. This in turn leads her to struggle with the question as to why God in his wisdom did not prevent sin from appearing in the world in the first place. In response, she receives the first of a series of locutions within this revelation which introduces one of the best known themes of Julian's *Revelations*:

Jesus ... answered with these words and said: Sin is necessary, but all will be well, and all will be well, and every kind of thing will be well.

(pp. 224–5)

In subsequent locutions within this revelation, the theme is repeated and Julian is reassured that her sin will be transformed:

I shall completely break down in you your empty affections and your vicious pride, and then I shall gather you and make you meek and mild, pure and holy through union with me.

(pp. 226–7)

Julian continues to struggle with how things can be well, finding it impossible to believe. The only answer that she receives here is that 'What is impossible to you is not impossible to me' (p. 233). The final chapter dealing with this revelation concludes with an affirmation of the need to hate sin, but to live in loving longing for God and in love for our own souls, and for one another.

The text concerning the **fourteenth revelation** initially addresses the nature of prayer, and much of this is a contemplative reflection upon a locution that is recorded in the initial chapter, Chapter 41:

> And our Lord brought all of this suddenly to my mind, and revealed these words and said: I am the ground of your beseeching. First, it is my will that you should have it, and then I make you to wish it, and then I make you to beseech it. If you beseech it, how can it be that you would not have what you beseech?
>
> (p. 248)

By Chapter 50, having 'seen' that though human beings are sinful, yet God is never angry (Chapter 46), that he is merciful and that he protects the soul and brings it peace (Chapter 48), Julian's contemplations lead her back to the vexed question of how she can reconcile her understanding of sin. On the one hand she sees that sin is blameworthy, and yet on the other hand her experience of the revelation has been that God does not show blame. She fears that she is in error and yet she finds it hard to doubt the truth of what she has 'seen'. Eventually, she finds the courage to ask:

> if it be true that we are sinners and blameworthy, good Lord, how can it then be that I cannot see this truth in you, who are my God, my maker in whom I desire to see all truth?
>
> (p. 266)

The answer to her question comes in the form of a vision of a lord and his servant which she understands as 'doubly shown', that is as being both 'shown spiritually, in a bodily likeness', and also 'more spiritually, without bodily likeness' (p. 267). The servant, eager to do his master's bidding, rushes off and falls headlong into a ditch. The master does not blame the servant, but rather wishes to reward him for suffering in the course of seeking to serve. Julian does not include this story in the short text, but her years of reflection lead her to find in it both an answer to her question of how to reconcile God's wisdom and mercy with the blameworthiness of sin, and also an understanding of the nature of the Trinity. For Julian, the servant is both Adam, and thus all humankind, and also Christ. Her reflections on this lead her to a theology of atonement, thus addressing the question that has so vexed her, and also to a theology of the Trinity, within which God as Trinity is understood as both father and mother.

Whilst Julian presents the parable as being a kind of double vision – of both bodily and spiritual kinds – it does also include a locution:

> Then this courteous Lord said this: See my beloved servant, what harms and injuries he has had and accepted in my service for my love, yes, and for his good will. Is it not reasonable that I should reward him for his fright and his fear, his hurt and his injuries and all his woe? And furthermore, is it not proper for me to give him a gift, better for him and more honourable than his own health could have been? Otherwise it seems to me that I should be ungracious.

> (pp. 268–9)

At the beginning of the **fifteenth revelation,** in Chapter 64, Julian 'had great longing and desire of God's gift to be delivered from this world and from this life' (p. 305). In response, she receives from God another locution:

> Suddenly you will be taken out of all your pain, all your sickness, all your unrest and all your woe. And you will come up above, and you will have me for your reward, and you will be filled full of joy and bliss, and you will never again have any kind of pain, any kind of sickness, any kind of displeasure, no lack of will, but always joy and bliss without end. Why then should it afflict you to endure for a while, since it is my will and to my glory?

> (p. 306)

After this she describes (in the long text) a vision of a formless body lying on the earth, 'as it were a devouring pit of stinking mud' (p. 306). From this body arises a beautifully formed child who ascends to heaven. Thus, the locution and the vision confirm to

Julian that suffering here on earth is to be accepted and endured out of love for God, and with hope of heavenly bliss to come.

Julian tells us (pp. 180, 310) that during the course of the first fifteen revelations she was free from pain. After the fifteenth revelation the symptoms of her illness return and she is visited by a priest. She tells him that she has been 'raving', in response to which he initially laughs. When Julian tells him of how she saw the crucifix bleeding, he becomes serious and Julian feels ashamed and guilty, fearing that by referring to what happened as 'raving' she was showing that she did not believe what God had revealed to her. Following this, there appears to have been a period of several hours about which Julian says only:

> I lay still until night, trusting in his mercy, and then I began to sleep.
>
> (p. 311)

In her sleep, she has a frightening dream of the devil. She is careful to distinguish this experience from the other 'showings', emphasizing that whereas this experience came during sleep none of the others did. However, when she wakes she sees smoke coming in at the door with 'great heat and a foul stench' and thinks that there must be a fire. Those who are with her assure her that they cannot smell anything and, being reassured, she

> was brought to great rest and peace, without sickness of body or fear of conscience.
>
> (p. 312)

The **sixteenth and final revelation** is a spiritual vision in which she sees her own soul:

> I saw the soul as wide as if it were an endless citadel, and also as if it were a blessed kingdom, and from the state which I saw in it, I understood that it is a fine city. In the midst of that city sits our Lord Jesus, true God and true man, a handsome person and tall, highest bishop, most awesome king, most honourable lord.
>
> (p. 313)

Following further description of this vision, and some reflections by Julian concerning it, she then relates a final locution, which she again describes as words revealed 'without voice and without opening of lips'.

> Know it well, it was no hallucination which you saw today, but accept and believe it and hold firmly to it, and comfort yourself with it and trust in it, and you will not be overcome.
>
> (p. 314)

Although this is the final revelation, and she says that 'soon all was hidden, and I saw no more after this', it is followed by a further encounter with the devil. This time she is not specific about whether or not she is asleep, but she refers to the heat and stench which previously she experienced when she was awake. This time she also hears a conversation

> as if between two speakers, and they seemed to be both talking at once, as if they were conducting a confused debate, and it was all low muttering. And I did not understand what they said, but all this, it seemed, was to move me to despair, and they seemed to be mocking us when we say our prayers lamely, lacking all the devout attention and wise care which we owe to God in our prayer.
>
> (pp. 315–16)

Despite the fact that Julian has referred to the locution of the sixteenth revelation as being 'the last words', she says here that God comforts her amidst the 'commotion' caused by the devil 'by speaking words aloud' (p. 316). She does not say what words were spoken, but this appears to be the only place where she is completely explicit that the voice that she hears is spoken out loud. She spends the rest of the night with her eyes focused on the crucifix, speaking of the passion, 'repeating the faith of Holy Church' and 'clinging to God with all my trust and strength' (p. 316). By morning the sights and sounds had gone, and only the stench persisted for a while.

Julian tells us that she continued to reflect on the meaning of the revelations, and that fifteen years later

I was answered in spiritual understanding, and it was said: What, do you wish to know your Lord's meaning in this thing? Know it well, love was his meaning. Who reveals it to you? Love. What did he reveal to you? Love. Why does he reveal it to you? For love. Remain in this, and you will know more of the same. But you will never know different, without end.

(p. 342)

Julian's visions and voices

Julian distinguishes between bodily visions, words formed in her understanding and spiritual vision. She says little about this taxonomy, and in places she appears to blur its boundaries.

Of bodily visions she says 'I have said as I saw, as truly as I am able' (p. 322), and of the words formed in her understanding she says 'I have repeated them just as our Lord revealed them to me' (p. 322). This conveys a sense of visual images which she has described as best she can in words, and of words which she has repeated faithfully. It does not clarify whether she saw these visions and heard these words in external space, or within her own mind, and it does not clarify whether or not the words were heard out loud. The only unambiguous example of a voice heard out loud is that of the devil, following the sixteenth revelation. Several of the early visions are concerned with the crucifix that she has been given, which is clearly a real object firmly located in external space. When she sees Christ bleeding on the cross, or his face discoloured, we may therefore wonder whether these experiences are technically illusions, or acts of imagination, rather than hallucinations or visions. For example, Molinari (1958) suggests that Julian's bodily visions may be explained as:

a Divine action on the imagination or internal senses, stirring up and uniting perceptions already received through sight or hearing.

(p. 63)

However, it is not Julian's purpose to clarify such things, and we must accept that we simply do not have firm evidence upon which we can base any definite conclusions.

The spiritual visions are a little more complicated. In Chapter 9, she says 'I may not and cannot show the spiritual visions as plainly and fully as I would wish' (p. 192) and in Chapter 73, she says 'I have told a part, but I can never tell it in full' (p. 322). This mystical ineffability clearly places these experiences in a different category. However, it does not appear to remove all verbal or visual reference. Thus, in the first revelation, Julian's spiritual vision of Mary is conveyed in words which concern her virtues, and which defy visual imagery, whereas in the sixteenth revelation, her spiritual vision of the soul is 'as if it were an endless citadel' which she is then able to describe in terms of largely visual images. The parable of the Lord and the servant is revealed 'doubly', both as a spiritual vision 'in bodily likeness' and also 'more spiritually, without bodily likeness'. There thus appear to be degrees of gradation of spiritual visions, some being more spiritual than others.

A similarity has been seen by some[3] between the three modes of revelation that Julian identifies and the three kinds of vision identified by Augustine of Hippo. As Molinari has shown (1958, pp. 60–70), whilst there is a tempting similarity at first glance, things are actually much more complicated than this superficial equivalence might suggest. Two of Julian's modes of experiencing her revelations are concerned with visual imagery, and one is verbal. If there is any equivalence, it is therefore on the basis (as Molinari does in fact suggest) that Julian has intermediate forms of vision, between the bodily and the spiritual. However, even then, there are serious questions as to whether, for example, Julian's bodily visions equate to Augustine's corporeal visions. In fact, they almost certainly do not, since the former (as suggested above) are at least sometimes imaginative, rather than being perceived through the bodily senses. Julian's spiritual visions, albeit only when they occur 'without bodily likeness', may well have a closer affinity to intellectual visions as understood by Augustine. However, the very fact that spiritual visions, for Julian, can occur in association with images, whereas intellectual visions, for Augustine, are by definition without images would seem to suggest that these modes

---

[3]See, for example, Robert Thouless, who suggests that Julian follows a 'classical distinction' of this kind (Thouless, 1924, p. 23); or Frederick Bauerschmidt, who rather more cautiously suggests that Julian's categories may be 'an indirect derivation of Augustine's scheme' (Bauerschmidt, 1999, p. 42).

of revelation are also different. All things considered, it would seem that Augustine and Julian adopted fundamentally different taxonomies of revelatory experience.[4]

The starting point for the revelations seems very clearly located in the realm of a visionary experience of the passion of Christ. Christopher Abbott (1997) has pointed out that this experience is in fact conveyed primarily with just two 'animated pictures': the face and body of Christ first streaming with blood, and then dry and shrivelled. This imagery is, as Abbott has further argued, iconic rather than narratorial. It is thus distinct from other passion meditations of the period, albeit possibly (as Brant Pelphrey has suggested) reflecting something of the new approach to painting of the passion evident in Norwich at around this time. Whether or not these images are strictly hallucinatory is not Julian's concern. It is the meaning of the experience that matters to her, and not the form that it takes. However, it is associated with a variety of locutionary experiences which assist in elucidating the meaning in verbal form, culminating eventually in her realization (in her 'spiritual understanding') that the meaning is simply expressed in one word – love. Whilst the revelations may in one sense be summarized in this one word, there is also another sense in which both images and words prove to be far too limited to convey their meaning. Thus, in the twelfth revelation there are many words, but they surpass Julian's understanding and cannot be explained.

The revelations have a conversational quality about them. To some extent this overlaps with the range of normal experience of conducting an internal dialogue within one's own thoughts. In some places this takes the form of a process of reasoning and emerging understanding, whereas in other places specific words seem to come to mind. In other places, however, it moves away from a clear sense of these being Julian's own thoughts, to a clear identification of them, by Julian herself, as belonging to another agent. Sometimes this is because they are identified with a visionary figure (normally Christ). Sometimes it is less to do with the vision and more to do with a locution that arises in response

---

[4]See Molinari (1958, pp. 64–5) for further discussion. Molinari also distinguishes between intellectual visions which are or are not 'wholly preternatural'.

to a thought that Julian has. Rather than being classifiable into a small number of discrete categories, the locutions seem to be spread along a spectrum in which, at one end, they are clearly Julian's own thoughts, and at the other end they seem to her to be very clearly not her own thoughts.

Julian is thus nuanced, careful and subtle in the way that she describes and reflects upon the form that her visions and voices take. Her primary concern is with the meaning of the experiences, not their form (what we might call phenomenology), but she recognizes that she has been given something precious and she treats it with care. She neither wishes to claim too much, nor too little, for what she has experienced and she has pangs of guilt when she finds herself referring to these experiences as 'ravings'. Nonetheless, the fact that she says this at all shows her self-awareness. On the one hand these experiences are the 'ravings' associated with a serious illness (as we shall discuss below), but on the other hand they are not ravings at all – they are deeply meaningful 'showings' or 'revelations' – and ultimately Julian believes that they come from God.

Julian's illness

James McIlwain (1984) concludes that a differential diagnosis of the ascending paralysis that Julian describes[5] should include diphtheria, inflammatory polyneuropathy, tick paralysis and botulism. On balance, given the temporal chronology of the symptoms, and the rarity of tick paralysis in humans, the most likely medical diagnosis would appear to be botulism. Such a diagnosis allows for both the relative preservation of mental clarity that allows Julian to provide such a coherent account of her experience, and also the possibility that her mental state was yet in some way still altered by the infective process.

Analyses of Julian's mental state in the secondary literature are altogether confused and confusing. William Inge (1906) suggests that Julian's visions were in the context of

---

[5] Based on Chapter 3 of the long text. A slightly fuller account of this is given in Chapter 2 of the short text.

the state of hypnotism induced by steadily gazing at the Crucifix, on which also her thoughts were fixed with ardent longing. To fix the eyes steadily on one object seems to be almost a necessary condition of this kind of trance.

(pp. 57–8)

Robert Thouless (1924) suggests that, as a result of her illness

her normal mental life was weakened, and the scenes of the passion with which meditation had stored her mind welled up to the surface of consciousness and presented themselves with hallucinatory vividness.

(p. 25)

Conrad Pepler (1958) is surely correct when he says that 'there is no doubt that [Julian's] illness had played some part in [her] experience' (p. 312), but his subsequent analysis is undermined by his failure to distinguish between the possibility of a toxic confusional state (delirium) and what he refers to as 'a neurotic illness'. Having first asserted that there is reason to suggest the possibility of an acute neurosis, he concludes that Julian's revelations are 'not purely neurotic ravings' (p. 313). Unfortunately, this leaves a lingering implication that he believes that, if not purely neurotic, they must partly be so.

Paul Molinari (1958) finds that Julian's 'simplicity, freshness and modesty stand in complete contrast with what is usually considered typical of neurotic cases' (p. 29). His concern, however, seems to have been to clarify whether Julian's illness was either 'the effect of a neurotic or hysterical disposition or the result of a special activity of God' (p. 25). The presentation of these possibilities as mutually exclusive alternatives is unsatisfactory. As Grace Jantzen (2000, p. 79) points out, the assumption that God 'is to be considered the cause only of those things which otherwise are not accounted for' leaves us with a disruptive and unnatural view of God's intervention in human lives. Nor does it do justice to Julian's own understanding of the significance of her experiences.

Diagnoses of neurosis, and especially of hysteria, do not reflect current diagnostic systems. A more plausible diagnosis according to contemporary criteria would be of delirium,[6] and it is curious that this possibility appears to have been generally neglected in the literature. Whilst Julian's general appearance of clear consciousness might seem to weigh against this, there is some evidence that her level of consciousness fluctuates, and her affective and perceptual experiences would also be explicable on this basis. In asserting such a possibility, it is important also to assert that this need not be a reductive explanation which excludes any possibility of divine inspiration. Indeed, as Julian herself asserts, it is not the experiences themselves that are important, but rather their meaning. That the experiences initially arose during the course of an illness does not in any way undermine their significance. Indeed, given Julian's prior desire for such an illness, it might even be seen to affirm their significance. In any case, whatever the initial provocation and context, they provided food for thought for Julian over a period of two decades, and have been found valuable by others over a period of more than six centuries, and this in itself must suggest that they are not delirious 'ravings' of any ordinary kind.

Julian's theology and spirituality

As already noted above, Julian summarized her own understanding of the meaning of her revelations in just one word, 'love'. She is both clear and explicit that her visions do not mark her out as a special person. Rather, there may be readers of her book, and yet others who have never had such visions, who love God more than she does and who are loved more by God (Jantzen, 2000, p. 80).[7] But this does not diminish her conviction that her visions were given for the benefit of others, and that however unworthy she might be, yet she has to tell of what she has seen and heard so that others may benefit.[8]

---

[6]Code 293.0 in the 5th edition of the *Diagnostic and Statistical Manual of Mental Disorders* (DSM-5) (American Psychiatric Association, 2013, pp. 596–601), or code 6D70.0 in the 11th revision of the *International Classification of Diseases* (ICD-11) (https://icd.who.int/browse11/l-m/en#/http://id.who.int/icd/entity/1015017717).
[7]Chapter 9.
[8]Chapter 6.

The benefits of voices and visions

The benefit that Julian understands as arising from the visions is something that occupies her for many years and, notwithstanding her protestations of ignorance, it is clear that she thought deeply about them in the light of both scripture and the teaching of the church. In this context, the voices that she hears – whether immediately and literally, or more metaphorically and on reflection over a longer period – play a significant part in interpreting her experiences and conveying the meaning of them. Furthermore, her revelations have been found meaningful centuries later and continue to occupy saints and scholars who find value in reflecting on them after her. For Julian, truth is conveyed not only by experience (which she understands in this case as the work of the Holy Spirit) but also through the teachings of the church and the application of human reason (Jantzen, 2000, pp. 89–107).[9] A voice or a vision on its own is worth little, unless it is prayed and reflected on, thought about and critically engaged with in the context of the teachings of 'Holy Church'.

As a result of this prayerful, thoughtful struggling with the meaning of her experiences, Julian has left us with a complex and multifaceted work which is widely regarded as one of the great classic texts of Christian spirituality. One of the differences between the short text and the long text is an increased emphasis on Trinitarian theology (Jantzen, 2000, p. 108). For Julian, the simple meaning of the revelations, summarized in the single word 'love', is given its fullest expression in the Trinity (Jantzen, 2000, pp. 110–11). Whilst this is an entirely orthodox understanding, in which the love of God, Father, Son and Holy Spirit is manifested in the sufferings of Christ that were the focus of her visions, yet Julian brings to it some unusual, and even unorthodox, insights. In particular, her understanding of the motherhood of God, and especially of the motherhood of Christ, are profound and far reaching. Appearing in the long text, but not in the short text, these ideas appear again to be a fruit of her long reflection and meditation on what had been revealed to her. They are not without precedent in Christian scripture or tradition, for example, appearing in Isaiah 49.15 and in St Anselm's prayers, not to mention the *Ancrene Wisse* (*A Guide for*

---

[9]Chapter 80.

Anchoresses),[10] but Julian gives them completely new and original expression (Jantzen, 2000, pp. 115–24).

Julian is not sentimental or simplistic in her reflections on divine love. Indeed, they raise significant problems for her. If God is loving, why did he allow human sin, and how can his love be compatible with his anger? Julian finds some quite unorthodox answers to these questions too, notably that human beings at some level never completely assented to sin,[11] and that there is no anger in God.[12] In this, she might be understood as rather optimistic about both her theology and her anthropology (Wolters, 1966, p. 40),[13] but for all that her grappling with human sin and suffering, grounded in her own experiences and in her visions of the sufferings of Christ, can hardly be considered superficial.

Theology

Julian's long text thus leaves us with some important theological reflections, which continue to be debated to this day. Indeed, she reflects on some of the most important themes of Christian doctrine. On this basis, and notwithstanding her own protestations, she may be considered a significant theologian.[14] However, the long text is much more than a significant theological treatise, even if it is also this. Thomas Merton (1967, pp. 140–4) refers to Julian as 'one of the greatest English theologians ... *in the ancient sense of the word*' (my emphasis). In the early Christian world, and indeed for many centuries after, theology was considered not so much an academic discipline as an exercise of prayer, contemplation and an 'experience' of God. Merton thus recognizes that Julian's visions, and her reflections on them, are something more than theological insights that might arise from any ordinary process of human

---

[10]Savage, Watson and Ward (1991, pp. 132, 182); it would seem likely that Julian was familiar with this text – at least by the time she was writing the longer version of her own work (Peters, 2008).

[11]Chapter 37.

[12]Chapter 13.

[13]Williams (2014), in contrast, expresses a very different view, as discussed below.

[14]Feiss (2004) suggests that she 'was one of the most brilliant theologians ever to write in English' (p. 73).

reflection and intellectual engagement. Hugh Feiss refers to Julian as having a 'dilated heart' (Feiss, 2004, p. 70), by which he seems to mean that her visions in some way expanded the capacity of her soul/mind to grasp 'something of the greatness of God' (p. 60), in comparison with which all created things seemed small.

Rowan Williams (2014) suggests that Julian offers an 'anti-theology', by which he does not mean that she rejects systematic theological thinking, but rather that

> she is repeatedly turning upside-down the structure that unthinking theology takes for granted and challenging us to recognize that the perceptions and feelings induced by this unthinking theology are dismantled by letting yourself be shown the truth that all theology gestures towards.
>
> (p. 2)

In other words, Julian is inviting her readers to 'ask themselves whether they are asking the right questions' (ibid). This has important theological implications – for example – concerning the way in which we understand sin, atonement, theodicy and divine action in the world. However, echoing Merto and Feiss, it also has profound implications for our understanding of prayer.

Spirituality

Much has been written about Julian's spirituality and a full review of the secondary literature on this topic would require the writing of another book. Just a few selected examples will be taken up here as the basis for reflection upon the way in which *Revelations* draws its readers into a transformative and contemplative experience of prayer.

Oliver Davies (1992), comparing Julian's writings with those of Mechthild of Magdeburg, identifies a common transformative dynamic of the texts that these mystics have bequeathed to us:

> Having been touched and changed, then, in their deepest being, they give expression to this encounter through the medium of a text which itself becomes the means whereby other persons, the readers of the texts, are themselves drawn into their original experience.
>
> (p. 50)

For Davies, this transformative process is a manifestation of a 'noetic spirituality'. Julian's visions constitute divine revelations which she seeks both to communicate for the benefit of others and also to reflect upon herself. They are an 'exercise in the communication of truth' (p. 43) which reflects both the immanence and transcendence of God – thus partly comprehensible and partly incomprehensible in this world.

Helen McConnell (1993), taking a psychological approach to Julians' spirituality, suggests that Julian has gained a 'deep comprehension of the experience of shame and its effects on the human spirit' (pp. 395–6). McConnell understands Julian as speaking to the 'troubled human spirit' in a way which is particularly relevant to the needs of contemporary society, both challenging and comforting, requiring personal responsibility and yet also validating and affirming. For McConnell, Julian's remedy for shame is self-knowledge, which in turn leads us to knowledge of God:

> The profound psychological insight ... echoed by contemporary psychotherapy, is that while ego work remains to be done, one will not aspire toward truth, beauty or God.
>
> (p. 402)

Whilst this 'profound insight' might be questioned at one level – Julian does not offer anything approaching the kind of process of 'ego work' offered by contemporary psychotherapy – and she does affirm the traditional theological understanding of self-awareness of sinful human wretchedness – at another level McConnell's grasp of Julian's understanding of self-awareness is deeply perceptive. It acknowledges the paradox that although there is no wrath in God, God's nurturing, motherly, love still finds a place for discipline. As McConnell would have it, 'Above all, Julian affirms' (p. 404).

Taking a somewhat different, but also deeply psychological, approach Maggie Ross has described Julian's long text as an 'anagogic' text, which 'move[s] the reader from image to the event-horizon, where self-consciousness disappears and contemplation/beholding begins' (Ross, 2014, p. 75). Elsewhere, Ross imagines this contemplative journey as being one towards the centre of a circle. She sees the centre as being a point of complete silence, or of the 'outpouring humility of God whose centre is every where' (Ross, 1993, p. 341). In Julian's long text, Ross understands the centre of this circle as being represented by 'the fullness of "beholding", the place of *onyng*, the entry into God's poynte' (ibid). The text thus facilitates a change of perspective, an entry into silence, wherein it is possible to see that, notwithstanding present appearances from the circumference, all will be well.

The psychology that Ross offers is one of what might be called the unconscious, but which she prefers to call 'deep mind' (Ross, 2013) or 'apophatic consciousness' (Gillespie and Ross, 1992). Apophatic consciousness exists in continuum with 'discursive consciousness' but leads into a timeless, imageless and paradoxical world of contemplative self-emptying and receptivity.

Ross and Gillespie suggest that it is 'the strategy of [Julian's] text ... to make it the experience of her readers as well' (p. 59). This is a humbling experience, but ultimately it is one in which we discover not so much the meaning of Julian's text as the meaning of our own lives. For a Christian, this is a process of reading – and 'being read' – in relationship with God:

> God's comprehension of us encloses us as well as understands us. God is able to read us, no matter how flawed the text, and we seek to read God by allowing God to read us: this is the essence of *lectio Domini*.
>
> (Gillespie and Ross, 1992, p. 68)

Returning to Rowan Williams' notion of the anti-theology of Julian, the long text thus leads its readers into a process of self-examination and reflection. For Julian, prayer:

> is bound up with self-awareness, a keen eye for what is getting in the way of God's active being in us; and it will flourish as and when we stop trying to pray in order to make something happen on God's part and so become more fully aligned with the simple 'happening of God' which is going on unbrokenly in all reality.
>
> (Williams, 2014, p. 12)

Williams' take on Julian is also deeply psychological, but it is more a kind of pyscho-theology[15] than a psychotherapy, within which

> 'Revelation' is a therapy for theological language: it is the process whereby we come to grasp how many of our theological problems are about the unreflecting projection on to God of tensions and dead-ends generated in our own hearts by our own fears.

> (p. 12)

The place of voices in Julian's spirituality

The boundaries between spiritual experience and theology, voices and thoughts, are blurred in Julian's writing. In relation to her theology, Williams suggests that:

> [Julian's] writing reverses expectation by presenting itself as a kind of seminar conducted by the voice of Jesus: the difficult and 'dismantling' insights which are offered by that voice make for a protracted exploration, in the course of which certain problems disappear.

> (p. 2)

I would suggest that the 'seminar' that *Revelations* records is actually not just a theological seminar (nor do I imagine that Williams understands it in this way). It is a mixture of thoughts, voices and visions which variously take the shape of prayer, spiritual direction by Jesus and a kind of theological reflection by thinking out loud in Jesus' presence, within which some complex theological questions float to the surface. Jesus's voice is significant within the conversations that comprise this multi-modal seminar and also within what we may piece together by way of a wider understanding of Julian's spirituality.

We saw some of the more obviously conversational elements in Julian's experiences above, especially in the first, second, eighth,

---

[15]This is my term, not William's, but I think it does justice to the way in which I, as a reader, understand his reading of Julian.

ninth, eleventh, thirteenth and fourteenth revelations. It is, however, in the fourteenth revelation – in her exploration of the nature of prayer – that we gain most understanding of Julian's understanding of how these conversations come about.

In Chapter 41, at the beginning of her account of the fourteenth revelation, Julian tells us that 'our Lord revealed about prayer' (p. 248). This revelation comes about by way of a locution/voice:

> I am the ground of your beseeching. First, it is my will that you should have it, and then I make you to wish it, and then I make you to beseech it. If you beseech it, how could it be that you would not have what you beseech?
>
> (p. 248)

Prayer thus has a circular character – it originates in God, it emerges as a desire within the Christian for 'rightful prayer' and then it returns to God as a Christian 'beseeches' God for what he has ordained. In Chapter 43, Julian writes that prayer 'unites the soul to God' (p. 253) and that 'the soul by prayer is made of one accord with God' (p. 254). Julian understands this uniting, and becoming of one accord, with God as emerging from a form of contemplative prayer:

> for the whole reason why we pray is to be united into the vision and contemplation of him to whom we pray.
>
> (p. 254)

This experience of prayer takes the form of a loving desire for God which is ultimately only completely fulfilled in death:

> And so we shall by his sweet grace in our own meek continual prayer come into him now in this life by many secret touchings of sweet spiritual sights and feelings, measured out to us as our simplicity may bear it. And this is done and will be done by the grace of the Holy Spirit, until the day that we die, still longing for love. And then we shall all come into our Lord, knowing ourselves clearly and wholly possessing God, and we shall all be endlessly hidden in God, truly seeing and wholly feeling, and hearing him spiritually and delectably smelling him and sweetly tasting him.
>
> (p. 255)

Visions and voices, not to mention other experiences of God in prayer (feeling, smelling, tasting), in this life are thus a foretaste of something far more wonderful to come.

Julian's long text is remarkable for its ability to speak meaningfully to the human condition in a way that remains relevant more than six centuries after it was originally written. It is a text which requires and engenders a response, and into which one is drawn.[16]

---

[16]Cf Gillespie and Ross (2004, pp. 131–3).

3

Joan of Arc

Based upon the 1431 Rouen trial records, we know that Joan began hearing voices at the age of thirteen years. These voices were identified by Joan, primarily, as those of St Michael, St Catherine and St Margaret. The question of spiritual discernment – as to whether Joan's account of these voices as coming from God was to be believed – was a central question for the Rouen court, as it had been earlier for the dauphin and his advisors. Everyone had their own political, and thus conflicting, reasons for wanting to see the question answered in a way that was supportive to their own cause. However, theology was ostensibly at the heart of the discernment process and one of the leading theologians of the time, Jean Gerson (1363–1429), is said to have given his opinion on the matter.[1] Questions concerning diagnosis and canonization were to arise only many years later, largely in the twentieth century. This chapter will again follow the same pattern as the last two: attending first to a consideration of the voices that Joan heard, second to questions of illness and diagnosis and then, finally, to Joan's spirituality.

---

[1]Gerson is said to have been supportive of Joan, but there has been much debate as to Gerson's authorship of the key documents in this debate. See, for example, Fraioli (2003), Mazour-Matusevich (2003).

Joan's voices

The trial at which Joan gave her evidence[2] was not sympathetic to her cause. However, its proceedings were recorded in great detail, and thus we have more extensive documentary evidence concerning Joan than we do for almost any other comparable figure, albeit not written by Joan herself. Whilst the traditional view is that the trial was unjust and flawed, recent reviews of the evidence suggest that in fact some pains were taken to ensure correct process and recording that would withstand scrutiny, precisely because it was controversial, even at the time (Hobbins, 2005, pp. 13–26). The trial was an ecclesiastical inquisition, held under canon law, to investigate 'accusations' (actually public opinion) of heresy. The rules were therefore very different than any that we know in criminal or civil law today. Had Joan been acquitted, she would have been returned to the English and would probably have been executed anyway.

Joan reports early on in the trial that she believed her voices to be sent by God and that they protected her. Witnesses at the trial of rehabilitation, and other chroniclers, represent Joan as being guided by God. During the first few days of the initial trial, Karen Sullivan suggests, Joan moved from speaking about God to speaking about a voice (Sullivan, 1999, pp. 23–32). However, from the outset there are references to a voice (and to voices) as sent by God, and it is not clear that Joan ever claimed to have heard the voice of God directly. On the second day of her appearance before the court,[3] the record of the trial states:

> she declared that at the age of thirteen she had a voice from God to help her and guide her. And the first time she was much afraid. And this voice came towards noon, in summer, in her father's garden: and the said Jeanne had [not] fasted on the preceding day. She heard the voice on her right, in the direction of the church; and she seldom heard it without a light. This light came

---

[2]In fact, three trials were involved: a preparatory trial (9 January to 25 March), an ordinary trial (26 March to 24 May) and a trial for relapse (28 to 30 May).
[3]This was actually 22 February, her first day of appearance being 21 February. The weeks before this had been devoted to discussions of correct procedure, appointment of officers to the court and preliminary information gathering.

from the same side as the voice, and generally there was a great light. When she came to France she often heard the voice.

Asked how she could see the light of which she spoke, since it was at the side, she made no reply, and went on to other things. She said that if she was in a wood she easily heard the voices come to her. It seemed to her a worthy voice, and she believed it was sent from God; when she heard the voice a third time she knew that it was the voice of an angel. She said also that this voice always protected her well and that she understood it well.

(pp. 54–5)[4]

Two days later, on 24 February, at the next session of the trial, Joan was asked when she heard the voice come to her:

she answered: 'I heard it yesterday and today.'

Asked at what hour yesterday she had heard this voice, she answered she had heard it three times: once in the morning, once at vespers, and once when the *Ave Maria* was rung in the evening. And often she heard it more frequently than she said.

Asked what she was doing yesterday morning when the voice came to her, she said she was sleeping and the voice awakened her.

(p. 60)

On 27 February, the fourth session of her giving of evidence at the trial, Joan identified her voices as, variously, those of St Catherine (of Alexandria), St Margaret (of Antioch) and St Michael the Archangel (Barrett, 1931, pp. 68–9; Sullivan, 1999, p. 28).[5] Karen Sullivan points out that, according to legend, Catherine and Margaret shared important characteristics with Joan, not least that

---

[4]Quotations from the trial record, in English translation, and associated page references are from Barrett (1931) throughout.

[5]Although much less is on record about this, it would appear that she also saw Gabriel and other angels. See, for example, Barrett (1931, p. 119).

they were virgins who were faithful to God in the public arena and who were patient amidst suffering. Michael, similarly, in addition to his perceived association with the French royal family, shared Joan's role of mediating between God and human beings. As an angel, Sullivan suggests, Michael also transcended distinctions between male and female, rather as Joan did in her choice of clothes. Kenyon (1971, p. 839) notes that St Margaret, whose statue was to be found in the church in Domrémy, also dressed in male clothes and became a monk.

Sullivan suggests that, as the trial progressed, Joan appeared to become more confident in her identification of her voices with these three figures. She also suggests that we might consider that Joan 'collaborated with the clerics in the construction of the truth of her voices' (Sullivan, 1999, p. 32, see also Sullivan, 2014). Certainly there is a mismatch between the nature and motivation of the clerics' questions, and the nature and motivation of Joan's answers, but the conversation seems to result in an account of her experiences which Joan is willing to defend vigorously.

According to testimony given after her execution, Joan is reported to have said that her voices came 'chiefly when the bells were being rung at Compline or Matins' (Barrett, 1931, p. 336). Although the voices clearly came frequently without bidding, it also seems that she was able to summon them through prayer:

> Asked whether she calls St. Catherine or St. Margaret or whether they come without being called, she answered: 'They often come without my calling,' and sometimes if they did not come, she would pray God to send them.

> Asked whether she sometimes called them without their coming, she answered that she had never needed them without having them.
>
> (p. 100)

According to Joan's recorded testimony, the voices 'often' addressed her as '*Jeanne the Maid, daughter of God*' (Barrett, 1931, p. 102). In her testimony on 22 February, Joan claims that both the King of France (that is, the dauphin) and 'several others' also 'heard and saw the voices' (Barrett, 1931, p. 57). In response to later questioning, Joan said that she saw St Michael with her bodily eyes, and that she saw the faces of St Catherine and St Margaret. The latter two saints were described by Joan as wearing crowns, but she could not describe how they wore their hair.

Joan's own faith in her voices seems to have been unshakeable. Thus, on 31 March:

> And first she was asked whether she would submit to the judgement of the Church which is on earth in her every act and saying, whether good or evil, and especially in the causes, crimes and errors of which she was accused, and in everything concerning her trial: she answered that in all these things she would submit to the Church Militant provided that it did not command her to do the impossible. And by this it is understood she means the revocation of the things she has said and done (as the trial reports) in respect of the visions and revelations she claims to have from God. She will not deny them for anything in the world. What our Lord told her and shall tell her to do she will not cease doing for any man alive.

> (pp. 224–5)

According to Joan's testimony at the trial, the voice initially told her to be good and to go to church frequently. It subsequently told her that she should go to France, and gave instructions concerning her mission there and whom she should approach in order to pursue this mission. Although she is not completely explicit, it would seem that Joan must have been told by her voices to wear men's clothes:

> Asked if God ordered her to wear a man's dress, she answered that the dress is a small, nay, the least thing. Nor did she put on a man's dress by the advice of any man whatsoever; she did not put it on, nor did she do aught, but by the command of God and the angels.

> (p. 70)

Joan says in her testimony that the voices told her the location of a sword buried behind the altar in the church of St Catherine de Fierbois, and that a sword was duly found there and given to her.

Joan revealed in her testimony that St Catherine and St Margaret 'gladly heard her in confession, from time to time, and each in turn'

(Barrett, 1931, p. 81). The voices of St Catherine and St Margaret also told her that she would be wounded in the combat at Orleans. Joan says that St Catherine and St Margaret foretold her capture. She said that her voices forbade her from jumping from the tower at Beaurevoir, but that out of fear she disobeyed. Having done this, she says that she heard the voice of St Catherine encouraging her and told her that she would recover from her injuries. At her trial, the voice appears to have guided Joan in what she should and should not say, and generally given her encouragement and comfort. However, Joan also reported that she could not always understand what the voice said. There is also more than a little ambiguity in the record as to whether and how Joan was told by the voices what the outcome of the trial would be:

> the voices told her she will be delivered by a great victory; and then they said: 'Take everything peacefully: have no care for thy martyrdom; in the end thou shalt come to the Kingdom of Paradise.' And this her voices told her simply and absolutely, that is, without faltering. And her martyrdom she called the pain and adversity which she suffers in prison; and she knows not whether she shall yet suffer greater adversity, but therein she commits herself to God.
>
> (p. 115)

She also said that 'by revelation' she knew that the English would suffer great losses in France and that the French would be victorious.

Diagnoses

Until relatively recently, it was usually assumed in medical circles that the hearing of voices was a sign of mental illness (Cook, 2018). It is therefore not surprising that a wide range of diagnoses have been considered and offered in respect of Joan's voices. By no means all authorities have concluded that Joan was mentally ill. Thus, for example, Henker (1984) works systematically through the diagnostic options offered by the then new DSM III and concludes that she does not satisfy the criteria for any of them. However, since the early twentieth century, there has been much speculation about a range of diagnostic possibilities, many of them reflecting the diagnostic fashions of their times.

One of the earliest published medical opinions was that of a doctor, G. Dumas, published as an appendix to Anatole France's 1908 biography of Joan.[6] Dumas noted that the famous French psychiatrist Charcot (1825–93) considered unilateral hallucinations to be common in hysteria. Taking Joan's initial account of the voice coming from her right as an indication that her voices might have been of this kind, but expressing reservation as to the reliability of this sign as indicative of such a diagnosis, Dumas went on to consider other characteristics of her hallucinations that might support a diagnosis of hysteria. He found some characteristics that he considered supportive of this diagnosis, notably what he referred to as Joan's 'clearness' and 'certitude'. However, he noted also that she disobeyed her voices when jumping from the prison tower at Beaurevoir, and this he considered to be uncharacteristic of hysteria. Eventually, Dumas reached an interesting conclusion, within which psychiatric and mystical accounts of Joan's voices are interwoven:

> If there were any hysterical strain in her nature, then it was by means of this hysterical strain that the most secret sentiments of her heart took shape in the form of vision and celestial voices. Her hysteria became the open door by which the divine – or what Jeanne deemed the divine – entered into her life. It strengthened her faith and consecrated her mission; but in her intellect and in her will Jeanne remains healthy and normal. Nervous pathology can therefore cast but a feeble light on Jeanne's nature.
>
> (pp. 235–6)

Jacobson (1917) diagnosed Joan as suffering from multiple personality (with Catherine, Margaret and Michael identified as the other personalities) but also – in a somewhat self-contradictory fashion – affirmed her sanity and adaptation to her environment. MacLaurin (1919), having speculated that Joan's symptoms might be hysterical, yet thought it would 'not be far wrong' to consider her a 'visionary' and proposed various physiological explanations for her voices. For Money-Kyrle (1933), Jeanne's voices were understood

---

[6] For an English translation, see Stephens (1925, pp. 237–41).

as projections of her super-ego which reach hallucinatory intensity as a result of an hypothesized traumatic event in early life.

Perhaps most surprising are the diagnoses of Joan as suffering from a personality disorder. Henderson (1939) first proposed that Joan might have been what he referred to as a 'predominantly creative psychopath'. In Henderson's thinking, this variety of psychopathy was closely associated with genius, and for Henderson genius was

> associated with a state of mental imbalance, of heightened sensitivity, of disordered mental equilibrium due probably to the attempt to get square with reality and even more to dominate reality as a compensation for the inner unresolved conflicts which dominate conduct.
>
> (p. 97)

For Joan, then, it was giftedness, not madness, that was at the root of her voices. She experienced, rather:

> an exaggerated sensitivity, an ability to receive, record and express feelings and experiences which are foreign to the less gifted.
>
> (p. 102)

In another early paper, Bayon (1940) also proposed that

> the behaviour of Jeanne d'Arc was perfectly sane and that the formulation of her constructive ideas bore the impress of genius.
>
> (p. 170)

Her hallucinations, Bayon suggested, were

> largely the product of auto-suggestion based on intense religious beliefs.
>
> (p. 170)

In a not dissimilar vein, but seeing Joan as immature and suggestible rather than as a genius, Kenyon (1971) proposed that Joan had the gift of eidetic imagery, this perhaps being reinforced by long periods of fasting and prayer.

(p. 842)

It is perhaps surprising that more published opinion has not proposed that Joan suffered from schizophrenia. After all, she experienced religious hallucinations and whilst some of her beliefs might be deemed within the spectrum of normal religious experience, other content of her thoughts (her unshakeable belief in her divine mission, etc.) might well be considered delusional, at least by those who are unsympathetic and so inclined. However, she did not demonstrate formal thought disorder, or flattening of affect or any of the other negative symptoms of schizophrenia, and her ability to function effectively in life was not impaired.

In a very early paper, Ireland (1883) stopped short of offering a specific diagnosis, but argued that (as we now know, incorrectly) 'a hallucination is always something pathological' (p. 26). He clearly believed himself that Joan was deluded, but also recognized that (with one possible exception, as he saw it) Joan's delusions were in keeping with beliefs of the time concerning communication with a spiritual world: 'When the whole age was thus deluded, there is little wonder that Joan herself went with the current' (p. 26). Acknowledging that there was nonetheless room for difference of opinion, he left his readers to judge the case. In a slightly later expansion upon this paper (Ireland, 1885), he continued his argument in such a way as to make his own views more clear. On the one hand, he did not think that she fitted current diagnostic categories. On the other hand, he seemed sure that she was unwell:

Some have said that Joan was affected with theomania, with paranoia, or delusional insanity. Perhaps a separate variety would need to be made for her, just as natural orders have had to be made for one or two plants, while other orders include thousands. I do not know any insane person who was like her, but she was not quite sane.

(p. 83)

James (1930) speculated that, had Joan lived longer, she might have been diagnosed with dementia praecox, but expressed some reluctance about this, given her achievements. His diagnostic judgement was only swayed by what would now be considered rather irrelevant observations concerning her menstrual cycle. Allen (1975) confidently diagnosed Joan primarily on the basis of her 'voices', which he considered to be 'an almost certain indication of schizophrenia'. He was also concerned by her 'complete certainty of being right', particularly in respect of her voices, which he considered 'clearly indicate that she was deluded'. However, as Henker (1984) argues, Joan's voices and beliefs have to be assessed in the context of what he calls 'the extreme saturation of the religious atmosphere of the time'. Taking this into account, we might well agree with him that 'grounds for a diagnosis of schizophrenia are weak'.

A possible explanation for Joan's voices in the absence of other evidence of psychotic disorder might be that they represent complex seizures. Butterfield and Butterfield (1958) appear to have been the first to suggest that Joan's voices may have been the result of a brain tumour – a temporo-sphenoidal tuberculoma – secondary to bovine tuberculosis. Making no reference to this early paper, Ratnasuriya (1986) also proposed a temporal tuberculoma as the diagnosis. Responding to Ratnasuriya, Nores and Yakovleff (1995) query whether such a diagnosis is compatible with the remarkably good physical health that Joan appears to have enjoyed and her capacity to engage in armed combat wearing a heavy suit of armour.

Foote-Smith and Bayne (1991) have proposed that Joan suffered from temporal lobe epilepsy (TLE), and d'Orsi and Tinuper (2006) propose a diagnosis of idiopathic partial epilepsy with auditory features (IPEAF). Both papers note that Joan's voices appear to have been evoked by auditory stimuli (the sound of church bells). Foote-Smith and Bayne identify the affective accompaniment of Joan's voices as indicating an ecstatic aura, whereas d'Orsi and Tinuper do not find evidence suggestive of ecstatic auras. Foote-Smith and Bayne also take up Ratnasuriya's proposal that a temporal tuberculoma may have provided the epileptogenic focus. Similar ideas have been taken up more recently by Muhammed (2013) and by Nicastro and Picard (2016) who also favour the diagnosis of IPEAF. In response, Kamtchum-Tatuene and Fogang (2016) have pointed out that the frequency of visual and auditory hallucinations experienced by Joan was much higher than would be expected in

IPEAF, that Joan did not experience seizures during sleep (sic)[7] and that hallucinations in IPEAF are usually devoid of coherent content. De Toffol (2016) has further queried whether the information available, from historical records of hostile interrogation, can be used in any case to support a medical diagnosis.

The breadth of diagnostic speculation is thus considerable, much of it reflecting historical trends and, with some notable exceptions, a lack of willingness to affirm the possibility that Joan's voices may simply have been within the range of 'normal' religious experience or, what we might now call, the hearing of voices in absence of any psychiatric diagnosis. In contrast to all of this, Tanya Luhrmann (2011), an anthropologist, has proposed that there are three patterns of hallucinatory experiences, one of which she actually calls the Joan of Arc pattern. She sees this as much less common than the other two patterns, one of which ('sensory overrides') is characterized by infrequent and non-distressing hallucinations, and the other one of which (psychosis) is associated with frequent and distressing hallucinations. The Joan of Arc pattern, according to Luhrmann, is associated with frequent and non-distressing hallucinations. Luhrmann suggests that Socrates may have been another historical example of this kind, and reports that she has encountered contemporary examples in the course of her fieldwork.

Joan's spirituality

In 1456, on 7 July, the verdict of the 1431 trial was nullified and Joan declared innocent. She was not canonized until 1920. In the processes leading up to the canonization, the evidence pertaining to Joan's life and experiences was again weighed in the balance, so that William Searle refers to this as her 'last trial' (Searle, 1976).[8] Was Joan to be admired merely for her military virtue, or was she, as her supporters argued, saintly in her kindness, charity and prayerful devotion to her faith? Or was her military prowess so amazing as to be understandable only on the basis of her receiving

---

[7]In fact, as d'Orsi and Tinuper (2016) have pointed out, a voice seems to have awoken Joan from sleep on at least one occasion.
[8]See also Kelly (2014).

supernatural aid? Outside the courtroom,[9] Searle points out, there were those who were much more sceptical. Was she presumptuous, naïve, manipulated by others, fanatical or deluded, patriotic more than virtuous?

Joan's voices have also been put on trial. Were they uninformative, even misleading more than helpful? In the court of historical-critical analysis, questions arise as to whether or not saints Catherine and Margaret ever actually existed. No historical evidence is available for either of them.[10] However, devotion to both was popular in the Middle Ages and Joan was probably familiar with them through pictures and statues in churches that she would have visited. Churches dedicated to St Catherine were within walking distance from Domrémy, and a fifteenth-century statue of St Margaret may be seen in the church in Domrémy today.[11] Both saints were known as virgins and martyrs and offered attractive role models for Joan. Veneration of the saints was an important part of the spirituality of Joan's time and, although there is no evidence that Joan ever had visions of, or heard the voice of, the Virgin Mary, her spirituality did include an element of Marian devotion (Astell, 2003).

Joan's spirituality was of her time in other ways as well. George Tavard (1997, p. 56) has suggested that 'aspects of her relation to God and Jesus evoke the *devotio moderna*', although he does not elaborate further on exactly what he has in mind here and we know little about Joan's inner life of prayer. We do know that she took a vow of virginity and that this meant more to her than merely sexual abstinence; referring, as she did, to 'virginity of body and soul' (Barrett, 1931, p. 57). We know that she was a frequent attender at church services and confession, and that most of what she knew about her Christian faith must have been derived from these sources (Kelly, 2003) as well as from her family. Joan clearly wished to remain loyal to the church, but the inward elements of her devotion – in particular her belief in her voices as a source of revelation – brought her into a political sphere of action on the one hand, and conflict with church authorities on the other (Kelly, 2003, Pinzino, 2003). As Ann Astell has noted, there is something

---

[9]And also within the courtroom – see ibid.
[10]See, for example, Benedetto et al. (2008, p. 133) and Cross and Livingstone (2005, pp. 306, 1041).
[11]Tavard (1998, pp. 76–7).

of a tension within Joan between the 'humble handmaid' and the 'virago' (Astell, 2003). Does this tension account for an apparent desire to emulate Mary on the one hand and St Michael on the other? The emphasis of her voices seems to be much more on the latter than on the former and, although Joan is rarely identified as a mystic, it has been argued that she did in fact follow a less common pattern of 'active' female mysticism (Barstow, 1985).

In concluding his monograph on Joan, George Tavard rightly argues that her spirituality 'cannot be neatly catalogued or classified' (Tavard, 1998, p. 169). He goes on to argue that her 'spiritual perceptions' drew her attention to matters of both heaven and earth which 'coalesced in her awareness of the divine presence' (Tavard, 1998, p. 169). Elsewhere, he argues that she is a paradoxical saint, but that the paradox lies within our assessments of her, and not within Joan herself.

> [Joan] was simplicity itself and there is no paradox without at least the appearance of duplicity.
>
> (p. 56)

This simplicity, which characterizes Joan's spirituality as understood by Tavard, was characterized by her awareness of her own 'littleness', her 'virginity of soul' (as evidenced in concern for a clear conscience), her self-understanding as 'daughter of God', her perceptions of light, the blurring of boundaries between God's Church in heaven and on earth, the need for both justice and charity, the inner urge to move forward and her invocation of God in prayer. All of these elements may indeed be found in Joan's spirituality, although we actually know very little about the content of her prayers other than in one response given during her trial, and in her moving calling out of the name of Jesus as the last words that she uttered before the flames consumed her on 30 May 1431. In these senses, Joan is simple, and her simplicity is attractive for its courage, honesty and singleness of purpose.

Tavard is also correct in asserting that many of the paradoxes – or perhaps, better, complexities – surrounding Joan's spirituality arise from our assessments and interpretations of her, and not from Joan herself. There has been a whole field of study devoted to issues of 'reception' of Joan of Arc. In Marina Warner's *Joan of Arc, The Image of Female Heroism*, for example, we learn how

Joan has inspired numerous causes over the half a millennium or more since her death, including feminism, nationalism, socialism and Catholicism, often with tenuous connection to the historical realities of her story. Much of this is concerned with the projections of others onto Joan and tells us more about those who adopt her as their saint or heroine than it does about Joan herself. However, Warner also draws attention to the internal contradictions: Joan's perceived worldliness, her support for the crusades,[12] her impatience with diplomacy and her disregard for the rules of chivalry (Warner, 2013, pp. 144–67). Joan's unshakable conviction was both a strength and a weakness in respect of her sense of divine calling:

> Joan had the hero's essential quality, an unshakable conviction in her rectitude and the rectitude of all her motives, her passions and her enterprises. This is what she meant when she said she came from God: she came from true rightness that could never slip into wrong. But such commitment is often seen as fanaticism and even madness by the opponents of a cause; and in Joan's case, her chivalry, like her voices and her dress, formed part of her aberration.
>
> (p. 167)

Similarly, Joan's simplicity, which can seem so appealing, creates its own problems. Her innocence, her 'littleness' (to use Tavard's word), arise not from wisdom, knowledge and experience but from an unwillingness, or perhaps an inability, to attend to complex political and theological realities. As Warner goes on to argue, Joan is a 'child saint' who provides a 'simple image of perfection' (p. 249) which eliminates complications, moral dilemmas and ambiguities:

> This feels reassuring. Creating simplicity often makes the heart leap; order has been restored, the crooked made straight. But order is understanding that things cannot be made simple, that complexity reigns and must be accepted. Infantilism is extrinsic to Joan, however young she was; it is projected upon her by adults who fear the absence of such clear and simple goodness in themselves and through themselves, who fear its disappearance

---

[12]See also DeVries (2003).

in everyone and therefore feel a need to experience it in reality by finding it in someone who lived.

(pp. 249–50)

Joan's simplicity may therefore be just another projection by us onto Joan, another kind of hagiography, as we seek to reassure ourselves that true saintliness is possible amidst a complex and dangerous world. The simplicity of the historical Joan of Arc almost certainly included a degree of naivete, as well as its own internal paradoxes, but this does not mean that she was not courageous, honest and single minded in her pursuit of what she believed was the divine mission communicated to her by her voices. Indeed, it may be precisely these virtues that make her susceptible to adoption by so many causes. Siobhan Nash-Marshall (1999), in her spiritual biography of Joan, has suggested that her spirituality was one of a divinely inspired quest. This quest raises complex questions for us (as it did for Joan's inquisitors) about the theology of nationhood, but for Joan it was in principle a very simple one.

Simplicity is, ironically, not a simple concept (Payne, 1993, 2005) and Joan did not live in simple times. On the one hand there is a simplicity, or perhaps we should say pseudo-simplicity, which reflects only naivete, or an over-simplification of things that tends towards the simplistic. This is clearly not what is held up within Christian spirituality as being admirable. On the other hand, there are simplicities such as those of lifestyle, mystical prayer or the love of God which reflect a dedication to God above all else, and which are associated with Christian maturity (and this is not necessarily encountered only in old age – as demonstrated by the lives of saints such as Thérèse of Lisieux). Joan's simplicity of focus upon a particular political mission, communicated by voices that she did not seem to question or subject to critical spiritual discernment, sits uneasily with the latter, and might easily be understood as the former. This said, we should not forget that her dying breath was devoted simply to calling on the name of Jesus. For this alone, we should surely remember her with love and affection, but that does not mean that we should be as uncritical of her voices as she apparently was.

In search of a more critical account of Joan's spirituality, it is illuminating to compare Joan with Thérèse of Lisieux, another 'child saint', who formed a great affection and admiration for her 'sister' Joan of Arc. Thérèse's spirituality was characterized by 'littleness', and she took the religious name of Thérèse of the Child Jesus. Thérèse did not hear voices. She had, however, read John of the Cross. Encountering suffering and trials towards the end of her life in various forms, she interpreted these in terms of her own experience of a 'dark night' of spiritual experience. Thérèse's affection for Joan of Arc was initially very idealistic and, when she wrote a play about Joan for performance in honour of her prioress in January 1894, in the same week in which Joan was declared venerable by Pope Leo XIII, Thérèse projected much of herself onto the character of Joan (Gaucher et al., 2008, p. 63). Exactly one year later, another play written about Joan by Thérèse was performed in the Lisieux Carmel. Reflecting back on this, as she approached her own death in 1897, Thérèse identified with Joan in prison (Gaucher et al., 2008, p. 137). The emphasis had moved from triumph to passion, from idealism to an encounter with darkness and death. Whilst all of this tells us more about Thérèse than about Joan, and we are told relatively little about Joan's final days in prison in any extant documents, we might discern the same evolution of emphasis in Joan's spirituality. Ultimately it is Joan's calling on Jesus from the flames that tells us more about the depth of her spirituality than it is her military triumph at Orleans.

4

Towards a more meaningful psychiatry

Over the last thirty years or more, spirituality has increasingly been recognized as an important clinical concern for psychiatrists (Cook, 2022c). This is, in part, because users of mental health services, traditionally referred to as patients, have increasingly been empowered to speak out about their concerns and have made clear that spirituality is important to them. Whereas historically psychiatry, influenced by Freud, behaviourism and biological neuroscience, has been antagonistic towards religion, increasingly it is reassessing its stance (Cook, 2022c). Research has shown that spirituality and religion provide positive coping resources and are associated with lower rates of psychiatric morbidity and better outcomes following treatment. Research has also yielded evidence of benefits associated with spiritual interventions such as mindfulness and forgiveness therapy, and spiritually/religiously integrated forms of psychotherapy.[1] Most importantly, however, it is virtually impossible to disentangle the spiritual and the psychological dimensions of human experience. For patients who identify as spiritual or religious, it is difficult to talk about emotional well-being without reference to spiritual well-being, and vice-versa. As psychiatrists are increasingly encouraged to take a patient-centred approach to clinical practice, things that are important

---

[1] The research literature is huge but, for a clinical overview, see, Cook and Powell, 2022. For overviews of scientific research studies, see Rosmarin and Koenig, 2020 and Koenig, 2018.

to patients – including spirituality and religion – have to become things that are important to psychiatrists (Person-Centred Training and Curriculum (PCTC) Scoping Group and Special Committee on Professional Practice and Ethics, 2018).

These changes have not been without controversy and have given rise to professional debate, notably about the nature and location of appropriate professional boundaries (Cook, 2013a). These debates have, in turn, led to the development of recommendations and guidelines for good practice which address such things as the need for a sensitive approach to clinical assessment, the avoidance of proselytizing, professional education and the importance of collaborative working with chaplains and faith leaders (Cook, 2017). There are, however, more intangible concerns which are not so easily dealt with. Psychiatry, at least etymologically, is concerned with 'treatment of the soul' (Cook, 2022a, p. 387), but there are diverse understandings of exactly what the soul is (e.g. is it the same as 'mind', or is it something different, such as 'spirit'?) and this description of psychiatry sounds superficially similar to what the world's major spiritual and religious traditions also seek to address. In practice, psychiatry, as a branch of medicine, is primarily scientifically informed and seeks to bring about the relief of suffering. It is therefore problem orientated but also person-centred. Spirituality and religion, in contrast, are philosophically and theologically informed and pursue more intangible, often transcendent, objectives. They are concerned particularly with relationship, and with finding meaning. Usually, although not always, they are theologically centred.

When we turn to phenomena such as the hearing of voices, it is immediately apparent that there is scope for conflict and misunderstanding of worldviews. Psychiatry (albeit now more aware than previously of the potential normality of voice hearing) will be more likely to see such experiences as signs or symptoms of an underlying disorder. Spirituality and religion will be more likely (whether or not such phenomena are in fact pathological) to see them as spiritual/religious experiences. Given that psychiatrists are rarely well versed about spiritual/religious experiences, and chaplains, clergy and faith leaders are rarely well informed about mental health, a voice may easily be misinterpreted. It may be wrongly understood as evidence of psychopathology, when it is in fact a normal experience within the faith community of the person concerned, or else wrongly overlooked as a sign of mental disorder because mistaken for a spiritual experience within that faith community. This should not be taken to suggest that such experiences must necessarily be either one or the other, either symptoms of illness or spiritual experiences. Such things are not mutually exclusive. For example, in recent research in the Netherlands, people suffering from episodes of mania had spiritual experiences as a part of their illness which they valued and affirmed long after their recovery (Ouwehand et al., 2018; Ouwehand, 2020). To disregard the spiritual significance of such experiences represents a form of epistemic injustice (Cook and Cullinan, 2022).

Psychiatry, a specialty in medicine which dates back only to the beginning of the nineteenth century (Shorter, 2005, pp. 232–3), thus finds itself at a very significant juncture in its history. Whilst for some time it has wrestled with internal tensions over the extent to which it has a primarily biological or psychological focus in its understanding of mental disorders (Clare, 1980; Luhrmann, 2000), the former focused on brain and the latter on mind, now it faces a further challenge. Will it embrace the importance of spirituality as something that is central to understanding the human condition, or will it reaffirm its research evidence base, its scientific approach and its traditional boundaries? If the former, then we might wonder how it will go about the interdisciplinary endeavour that this will entail. If the latter, then we might well ask, at what cost will this be to patients whose care will be fragmented between medical and spiritual professionals, neither of whom have a full understanding of their condition?

Spirituality, religion and the humanities

The present challenges facing psychiatry are embedded within a wider fabric of social change. Attitudes to religion, and the observance of religious practices, have changed enormously since the fifteenth century, and especially over the last century, in the western world. While religious affiliation remains the norm, with atheism and other forms of 'non-religion' in a small minority worldwide, in western nations – not least the UK – religious observance has declined at the same time that religious plurality has increased (Cook, 2022b). Increasing numbers of people (including, of course, users of mental health services) define themselves as 'spiritual but not religious' (SBNR) or else draw, in a 'pick and mix' kind of way, on beliefs and practices deriving from a variety of religious traditions. Spirituality has come to be distinguished from religion even though, worldwide, the spirituality of most people is still deeply embedded in their religious identity.

Spirituality is notoriously difficult to define. There are many definitions, and yet there is no commonly agreed definition. The theme of relationship – with self, others and a wider reality – is commonly observed as being important. For some, it is the acknowledgement of a transcendent reality that is at the core of the concept, and yet many of the newer expressions of spirituality have a strong focus on immanence (Cook, 2013c). An example of a definition which aspires to being inclusive of this diversity of understandings may be found in the Royal College of Psychiatrists' position statement, *Recommendations for Psychiatrists on Spirituality and Religion*:

> a distinctive, potentially creative, and universal dimension of human experience arising both within the inner subjective awareness of individuals and within communities, social groups and traditions. It may be experienced as a relationship with that which is intimately 'inner', immanent and personal, within the self and others, and/or as relationship with that which is wholly 'other', transcendent and beyond the self. It is experienced as being of fundamental or ultimate importance and is thus concerned with matters of meaning and purpose in life, truth, and values.
>
> (Cook, 2004, 2013b)

Whilst spirituality is a useful concept within the consulting room, being inclusive of diversity and understandable by people of all faiths and none, it has proven less useful in healthcare research. The concept of spirituality is less easily operationalized than religion/religiosity and is easily confounded with psychological variables (Koenig, 2008). It has been argued that research on mental health and well-being should therefore focus on religion/religiosity rather than spirituality. This may well be helpful in some countries, and we certainly need more research on religion and mental health. However, religion is also a difficult concept to define and measures of religiosity that work well in the context of populations of high religious plurality are less easily constructed. It is not impossible to conceive of measures of spiritual practice ('spiritosity' (Cook, 2022c, pp. 11–12)) that work across different religious traditions, and are also applicable to those who are SBNR, but valid and reliable measures of this kind are currently more an aspiration than a reality.

The concept of spirituality is itself a part of a broader recognition within the world of mental healthcare that something more is needed for truly person-centred clinical practice. It overlaps with concepts such as recovery, compassion and values-based practice (Person-Centred Training and Curriculum (PCTC) Scoping Group and Special Committee on Professional Practice and Ethics, 2018). The concept of recovery, in particular, seeks to move away from expectations of good outcomes defined in a narrowly medical way and looks to the broader context of the way in which patients recovering from episodes of mental illness find meaning and purpose, and function in social relationships (Leamy et al., 2011; Jacob, 2015).

Spirituality might also be seen as a part of the broader field of medical humanities although, curiously, theology and religious studies – disciplines within the domain of the humanities – are often under-represented in medical humanities research (Pattison, 2007). The medical humanities seek to broaden understanding of the human condition by drawing on literature, history, philosophy and other non-scientific disciplines to enrich the vision of the human condition. In each case there is an enhanced emphasis on subjectivity, meaning and human values. We might well ask whether this broader searching for a model of understanding which seeks for something more holistic, inclusive and embracing of a broader vision of the human condition is in fact spirituality by another name. Within psychiatry, the medical humanities help to focus clinicians' attention on the importance of such things as empathy, narrative and the human search for meaning (Datta, 2016; Schlozman, 2017; Dosani, 2021). The critical medical humanities are also helpful in 'putting past and present into conversation' (Saunders, 2016, p. 411).

Boundaries, controversies and secularity

For some, the broadening of perspective that sees spirituality as an important dimension of the human condition, to be sympathetically addressed within the clinical practice of psychiatry, is welcomed as a 'paradigm shift' (Culliford, 2011, pp. 91–101). Some would wish to see the prevailing biopsychosocial model replaced by a biopsychosocial-spiritual model of care (Kuhn, 1988), but it is arguably preferable to emphasize the place of spirituality within each of the biological, psychological and social dimensions of care, and not as a potentially separable fourth dimension. On the other hand, there are those who have misgivings over the movement to incorporate spirituality within psychiatry (Poole and Higgo, 2011). Whilst it would be foolish to overgeneralize, and the debate has ranged far and wide, these concerns and controversies might be said to fall largely under four headings:

Boundaries

Secularity

Potential for harm

Scientific evidence

The principal professional **boundary issues** concern expertise (psychiatrists are specialists in medicine, not in spiritual care) and the boundary between the personal and the professional domain of the clinician (dangers of proselytizing or other impositions of the view of the clinician on the patient). Whilst these are both very real concerns, neither is conclusive. If spirituality is properly a part of psychiatry, then it should be taught as such, and failures of past medical education should not be allowed to dictate proper practice for the future. Similarly, the possibility of malpractice (e.g. proselytizing) should not dictate good practice. We do not fail to discuss sexuality with patients because of the dangers of sexual abuse. Why should we exclude discussion of spirituality because of the possibility of spiritual abuse?

There are also conceptual boundaries. Some would argue that spirituality and psychiatry are distinct disciplinary domains and should therefore be dealt with by different professional groups, but there are also counterarguments. Who is to say that, for example, a feeling of being distanced from God is a spiritual rather than a mental health problem? Are mind and soul separate concerns or, as many might now argue, is the psyche – the mind and the soul – actually the concern of both psychiatry and spirituality? However one may answer these questions, it is clear that spirituality and psychiatry have many concerns in common and that the boundaries between the two are at least blurred. Trying to artificially separate them, as though they were separate concerns in life, so that they can be dealt with by different professionals, is not helpful to an integrative and holistic view of patient care.

Some would argue that **secularity** provides a safe space for the clinical interface, and that the introduction of spirituality/religion into professional practice is an unhelpful blurring of boundaries. However, secularity is not neutral and is often perceived as being antagonistic towards religion, especially in relation to psychiatry. Mental health service users have complained that they cannot discuss their spiritual/religious concerns with their clinician for fear that these issues will be understood as a part of the pathology rather than the solution (Macmin and Foskett, 2004). Proselytizing for atheism or agnosticism is no less a professional ethical concern than proselytizing for a particular religious stance.

There are legitimate questions to be asked about the **harm** that might arise, in at least some circumstances, as a result of spiritual/religious beliefs and practices on the one hand, or professional practice on the other. Religion may foster a sense of guilt and may be a cause of anxiety, as well as a basis for finding forgiveness and peace. Inappropriate or insensitive exploration of spirituality/religion by professionals may be a cause of distress. Again, these concerns would seem to be arguments for better training and more research, rather than reasons for keeping spirituality and psychiatry at a distance from one another.

Finally, there are legitimate debates about the strength of the **scientific evidence** and, it must be acknowledged, some of the research – especially the earlier research – supporting a positive relationship between religious affiliation and mental well-being has been of poor methodological quality (Bonelli and Koenig, 2013). The strength of the correlations is also much less than sometimes acknowledged. No argument is being made here against more and better research. Nor is it helpful to argue for more of a benefit from spiritual/religious practice than is actually borne out by the evidence. Equally, it is not helpful to deny benefits that have been reliably demonstrated by the now very large evidence base.

Spiritually significant voices

The hearing of voices (auditory verbal hallucinations according to the terminology of psychology and psychiatry) provides one particular phenomenological context within which debates about the place of spirituality and religion (and the humanities more widely) in psychiatry are conducted. Spiritual voices are a point of connection where a particular kind of voice hearing, voices evaluated by those who hear them as 'spiritually significant', may help us to better understand some of the broader issues about the importance of meaning making for patients, voice hearers and others who have spiritual/religious experiences involving voices.

The identification of a voice as spiritual/religious may be based either upon the content of what the voice is understood to say – for example, a command to fulfil a divine instruction – or else upon the recognized identity of the voice – for example, that the voice is understood to be the voice of God, or an angel or saint. The attribution of spiritual significance is thus a subjective matter, residing largely in the experiences and understanding of the person hearing the voice. However, such voices may also be understood by others as spiritually significant. For example, in Hebrew scriptures, the hearing of the voice of God by the patriarchs and prophets has been affirmed by both Jews and Christians as divinely inspired and the voice (or a written record of what the voice reportedly said)[2] has effectively become scripture. Such voices – spiritually significant voices – are identifiable in scripture, in religious tradition and in contemporary spiritual and religious experience across various religions.

What might such voices have to teach us about the broader issues? The central proposal being made here is that they are important because they are a kind of focal point where the

---

[2]It is recognized that we have no sure way of knowing what the original experience of such voice hearers was like (the phenomenology of the voice), whether or not they literally heard a voice (as opposed to metaphorical or other literary devices employed by an author who might have described their experiences in this way) or even, in some cases (e.g. Abraham or Moses), whether they even ever existed as historical figures. However, the fact remains that voice-hearing experiences are significant in Hebrew, Christian and other scriptural traditions. For a fuller discussion, see Chapter 2 in Cook (2018).

phenomenology of a particular kind of perception-like experience intersects with biography, culture and sense of self in such a way as to be personally meaningful. All of this may, or may not, emerge from the context of a mental disorder. In a sense, the presence or absence of a mental disorder is quite irrelevant here, except insofar as the diagnostic paradigm and the machinery of mental healthcare may act to obscure, oppose or undermine the spiritual meaning and significance of the voice. The voice also may, or may not, emerge in a religious context, but this is not at all irrelevant, quite the opposite. The personal, cultural and social frameworks of religion may well shape the meaning of the experience very significantly. They may also, if ignored or misunderstood, contribute to misdiagnosis. Spiritually significant voices thus provide us with a kind of laboratory within which to study the relationships between subjective experience; personal, cultural and social context; and the construction – or discovery – of meaning.

Within this laboratory, empirical studies of a qualitative or quantitative kind have an important part to play. However, there is also value in historical, biographical and theological studies of texts that have been handed down to us within which spiritually meaningful voices have been described. Such texts give us a degree of distance from the human experiences to which they relate and therefore, perhaps, greater objectivity. We may imagine that such texts have been preserved because they describe relatively unusual, significant or otherwise interesting experiences. Other potentially similar historical experiences have, for a variety of reasons, either not been recorded or else the textual evidence relating to them has not survived. This makes the extant texts unusual, but the reasons for their preservation may in themselves be of interest. Texts that have survived will be more likely to include those thought especially valuable by reason of the spiritual wisdom that they impart, or their usefulness in spiritual/religious education or else that they provide evidence of the sanctity of the person (or persons) involved.

Amongst such texts are the *Book of Margery Kempe*, Julian's *Revelations* and the proceedings of the trials of Joan of Arc, the *Procès de Condamnation de Jeanne d'Arc*. Julian's *Revelations* give us a direct account of spiritually significant voices from the hand of the woman who heard them. Margery's *Book* is only one step removed, recorded by an amanuensis who appears to have been largely sympathetic to the voices and the woman who heard them. The

Procès were different in that they were recorded by unsympathetic scribes, in order to demonstrate that the voices were deceitful, and that the woman who heard them should not be believed.

Epistemic injustice

The preservation of revered historical texts concerned with spiritual voices thought to be exemplary, valuable and meaningful contrasts with the experience of many hearers of spiritually significant voices today, especially those who have a psychiatric diagnosis. Their experiences are often seen by others as evidence of psychopathology, without value to others and as meaningless. This is an example of epistemic injustice.

Epistemic injustice is concerned with the way in which a person's credibility as an 'epistemic subject' is undermined by others. That is, their claim to know things, and to be taken seriously in debate and discussion, is subject to prejudice. Their testimony is given less weight, and their interpretation of their experiences is doubted by others.[3] When related to spiritual voices this may be manifested as a reluctance on the part of others to believe that the voices are 'significant' or meaningful, other than as evidence of mental disorder. Thus, if the hearer of the voice believes that God has spoken, others may dismiss this as simply 'hallucinations'. If the voice hearer believes that the message they have received is of value to the wider church or community, others may contend that it should not be listened to and interpret the experience as deceptive or perhaps even as inspired by malign spiritual forces.

Although the concept of epistemic injustice is generally attributed to the relatively recent work of the philosopher Miranda Fricker, the phenomenon is by no means new. Thus, the genuineness of Margery Kempe's experiences was repeatedly, and unsympathetically, questioned by many (not all) of her contemporaries. The voice of epistemic injustice was heard in the Rouen trial of Joan of Arc, and perhaps also in the submissions of

---

[3]For helpful explorations of epistemic injustice in psychiatry, see Crichton et al. (2017) and Kidd et al. (2022).

the 'Devil's advocate' in the process leading to her canonization (Kelly, 2014). It is evident in the medical literature reviewed in the three preceding chapters, where the voices heard by Margery, Julian and Joan have often been attributed to medical diagnoses, thus discrediting their spiritual significance. Indeed, one might argue that any spiritually significant voice will always evoke a contrary voice in some form or another, if not in the mind of the individual, then almost certainly in the minds of others and in social discourse. The injustice is not the presence of contrary voices but, rather, in the extent to which those contrary voices take seriously and respectfully the epistemic authority of the voice hearer in relation to their own experience.

This seems to be a spiritual and epistemic dynamic with a long Christian history. In the second Genesis creation narrative, after the first man has heard God say, 'You may freely eat of every tree of the garden; but of the tree of the knowledge of good and evil you shall not eat, for in the day that you eat of it you shall die.' (Gen. 2.16-7). the voice of the serpent responds with, 'Did God say, "You shall not eat from any tree in the garden"?' (Gen. 3.1). The serpent's voice discredits and questions the voice that the man has understood as God's voice. The interpretation that the man and the woman have given to the voice that they understood as the voice of God is called into doubt. The voices of epistemic injustice echo the voice of the serpent in the garden in the Genesis narrative.[4]

This is not to say that the nature and meaning of voice-hearing experiences should not be critically questioned. Indeed, it is hard to see how such experiences can be taken seriously, and proper discernment of them exercised, if they cannot be questioned. The problem is rather the prejudice that is manifested in a presumption of incredibility, a prior assumption that the voice and the voice hearer are not to be taken seriously. It is about a failure to give a fair hearing, rather than the outcome of the hearing, but it is also about finding outcomes that are affirming, empathic and epistemically respectful towards the voice hearer.

---

[4] It is the dialogical dynamic by way of which voices are epistemically discredited that is of concern here, and this does not depend upon any particular, literal or mythological, reading of the Genesis text. For further discussion, see Cook (2018, pp. 59–60).

Problems with psychiatric accounts of voices

Not all of the medical accounts of the voices heard by Margery, Julian and Joan have been written by psychiatrists. Indeed, it is very interesting to note the breadth of interdisciplinary engagement in relation to historical-medical studies of these women. The secondary literature cited in Chapter 1, in relation to Margery Kempe, includes authorship by psychologists, historians, several English scholars, a social worker, a nurse and a pathologist. Only one of the co-authors of one paper (Freeman et al., 1990) is a psychiatrist, and another psychiatrist, Anthony Ryle, is quoted by Stephen Medcalf (1981). In Chapter 2, in relation to Julian of Norwich, none of the secondary literature cited is written by a psychiatrist, and only one author is a psychologist (Thouless, 1924). Other authors cited here include three priests and an ophthalmologist. Perhaps it is not surprising that most psychiatric attention has been devoted to Joan of Arc. Amongst authors cited in Chapter 3, there are seven psychiatrists, one psychologist, one psychoanalyst, five neurologists, one pathologist and four other medically qualified doctors, as well as one psychological anthropologist.

Psychiatry is an inherently interdisciplinary endeavour and so the interdisciplinary engagement of scholarship in relation to the three women who are the focus of this book is to be welcomed. It is interesting, but perhaps not surprising, that scholars in non-medical disciplines sometimes seem more confident than might be warranted in diagnosing – or refuting the diagnosis of – such conditions as hysteria. This diagnosis has always been problematic and is in any case replaced in current taxonomies with very differently defined categories. In relation to the putative physical diagnoses – forms of epilepsy, tumours and infectious diseases – the literature is appropriately dominated by authors who are pathologists, neurologists and other physicians. The diagnostic categories of psychiatry have always been much more controversial than are those of general medicine, and the medical model is much more vulnerable to critique in relation to most mental disorders.

There were no psychiatrists in the fourteenth and fifteenth centuries, but mental illness was still recognized as something that might be confused with spiritual experience (see Introduction).

Margery herself recognized that her post-natal illness was different than her later religious experiences, and Julian debated with herself (and with God) about whether or not her experiences were merely 'ravings' or, as we might say, delirium. Only in Joan's case does there seem to have been little or no serious contemporary consideration, by Joan herself or by others, of the possibility that her voices might have been due to mental illness. In all three cases theological and spiritual explanations were much more in the foreground than they would be today. The presumptions were largely weighted in the opposite direction to modern medical scholarship. 'Are there any reasons why these voices might not have been genuine spiritual experiences?' was the pressing question in everyone's mind, rather than 'What are the underlying medical explanations for these unusual experiences (which happen to have spiritual content)?'

Of course, there are going to be problems with any attempt to diagnose Margery, Julian or Joan across a gap of six centuries. As discussed in the Introduction, if any such quest is undertaken at all, we should be extremely cautious and tentative about any conclusions that we might draw from it. The biopsychosocial matrix of mental disorders is historically, as well as culturally, spiritually and religiously, contextualized and we simply do not have all of the information that we need to reach confident conclusions. However, that is not to say that we should not reflect with the aid of psychiatry and allied disciplines about the mental health of the past. To do so can be helpful as we reflect critically on the spirituality of mental disorders in our own time. We simply have to keep in mind the provisionality of our reflections, and exercise due humility in the conclusions that we draw.

A bigger problem is that any psychiatric account of voices, whether historical or contemporary, easily sounds reductionistic. This may come about because of a particular authorial perspective which emphasizes biology, or which prioritizes the form rather than the content of phenomenology, or else assumes a pragmatic atheism, or it may be simply that authors understandably endeavour to stay within their own disciplinary expertise and avoid drawing conclusions about the spiritual/religious meaning of the phenomenology which they are studying. Whatever the reason, silence about spiritual meaning tends to imply that it is unimportant, and explanatory or causal accounts based upon diagnosis are easily assumed to exclude spiritual/religious meaning as being (at best) of anything other than secondary importance. What is needed is a more integrative account, within which spiritual meaning is recognized as having a full 'place at the table'.

The failure to give spiritual/religious meaning its appropriate place at the table when discussing psychiatric accounts of voices is not just one of historical interest. It reflects a wider perspective on current clinical practice and reinforces a view that some patients have that psychiatrists simply see their spirituality/religion as a part of the psychopathology, rather than as a part of the solution. This in turn discourages such patients from seeking help from mental health services or, if they do, giving a full account of their spiritual concerns to the clinical staff who are caring for them. In fact, spiritual/religious coping is very important for such patients and is something that clinical staff need to be aware of. On the one hand, spiritual/religious struggles may need to be addressed sympathetically as a treatment objective, and on the other hand, positive spiritual/religious coping provides an evidence-based treatment resource which may be contributory to a good outcome.

There is a further problem affecting those who do give spiritual/religious meaning a place at the table. The spiritual and psychiatric perspectives, if not properly integrated, may easily be seen as mutually exclusive. For faith leaders, chaplains and mental health professionals who do take spirituality seriously, it is still often assumed that a particular experience – for example, the hearing of a spiritually significant voice – must either be evidence of psychopathology, or else a part of a 'true' spiritual experience. Criteria for making such a differential diagnosis have been published, further reinforcing this either/or account of things (see, for example, de Menezes and Moreira-Almeida, 2009). In fact, research shows that spiritual meaning and psychopathology may exist side by side during acute illness and that the meaningfulness of the experience is not negated by recovery from the episode of illness (Ouwehand et al., 2018). We thus need much better 'both/and' accounts of spirituality and mental illness.

Many – if not all – of these problems might be easily addressed by better interdisciplinary and interprofessional collaboration. However, the danger is that, within such collaborations, the scientific model assumes predominance. A perspective is needed within which the entanglements of psychiatry and spirituality are more clearly addressed. We shall return to this theme, below, but first it is important to ask what lessons psychiatry might learn from Margery, Julian and Joan.

What can psychiatry learn from Margery, Julian and Joan?

Standing back, at historical distance, what might psychiatry learn from the voice hearing and visionary experiences of the three women who have been the focus of this book, and from the various diagnostic exercises of psychopathography to which they have been subjected over the last century or more? I would not wish to suggest that the following proposals are in any way exhaustive. For example, they do not address the way in which the content of voice hearing and visionary experience are concerned with social traumas, such as war, plague and famine; nor have I addressed here the important impact of voice hearing upon the vocation of each of these women. I hope that readers will be able to think of other things that Margery, Julian and Joan may have to teach us. However, for the purposes of the present study, I would suggest that a number of important themes emerge concerning meaning making and its importance in social and cultural contexts.

1. Voices may be spiritually meaningful

Margery, Julian and Joan had meaningful voice-hearing and visionary experiences. Their voices and visions gave them a strong sense of vocation, divine guidance and purpose in life. Margery's voices and visions were affirmative of her relationship with God and gave her life meaning and purpose. Julian's voices and visions provided her with food for thought for twenty years or more and resulted in the writing of one of the classic texts of English spirituality. Joan's voices communicated to her a mission and purpose in life, which she and others understood to be from God, which changed the course of the Hundred Years' War.

We might disagree with the meaning that these three women found in their experiences, as did some of their contemporaries (particularly in the case of Margery and Joan). However, disagreements about meaning are, in a sense, affirmative of the importance of meaning. If something is important, we can disagree about what it means. It is worth discussing. If it is unimportant, we will probably not bother arguing about it.

Margery, Julian and Joan had very different approaches to spiritual discernment. Margery consulted far and wide and received diverse advice as to the spiritual authenticity of her experiences. We know little about Julian's life, although we may imagine it unlikely that she did not speak at length with her priest or confessor about her experiences (she did, after all, receive a visit from a priest during her near fatal illness). She certainly spent a long time in private reflection and prayer, a process which led her to expand upon and revise her initial account of the revelations that she received. Similarly with Joan, although we have no definitive account of the private counsel that she received, it would seem unlikely that she did not discuss her voices with a priest or confessor. Whether or not she did this, her voices were subjected to extensive, theological, political and public processes of discernment at Poitiers, in the various trials at Rouen and later at the Vatican in support of the processes leading to canonization. It is hard to imagine any other experience of voice hearing that has been subject to such extensive processes of discernment. It is also hard to imagine any other experience of voice hearing that has been subject to processes of discernment so distorted by epistemic injustice, political bias and other adverse external influences.

Spiritual discernment is primarily a prayerful and theological process and is not best served when distorted by other agendas. For Margery, we may wonder whether her inner need for affirmation and approval sometimes made it difficult for her to question her voices. The responses of others to her experiences were shaped both by the public theological controversies of the time and by reaction to her strong personality. For Joan, the inner convictions of calling were so strong that it is not clear that she ever really found herself able to question them. The nature of her quest was so politically controversial that it is hard to believe that she ever really received the dispassionate spiritual and theological hearing that her experiences deserved. Julian alone seems to have kept her experiences away from public scrutiny and to have pondered them at such length primarily within her own heart.

Margery, Julian and Joan are not typical of voice hearers in general, they were each exceptional women, but they do give cause for clinical and pastoral reflection on the meaning that might be found and affirmed in many other voice-hearing experiences. They also draw attention to the need for wise, confidential, person-centred and supportive processes of discernment. Why, we might ask, is spiritual direction (Saadeh et al., 2018) not offered more frequently in support of such an endeavour within mental health services?

2. Voices can help in spiritual coping

Margery, Julian and Joan lived at a troubled time in European history and did not have easy lives. Joan died young, after an eventful and controversial life in war and in the courtroom. Margery and Julian died as old women, the former having experienced conflict and danger at home and abroad, the latter after spending many years in an anchorage. When they were young women, Margery experienced a distressing puerperal mental illness and Julian nearly died of a physical illness. Joan's voices led to her execution. In different ways, each woman became closely acquainted with suffering and trials, and these sufferings were made meaningful and manageable, in large part, because of the voices that they had heard.

Van Tongeren and Van Tongeren (2020) argue that there are four core concerns that undermine existential meaning for people struggling with mental health issues: groundlessness, isolation, identity and death. Groundlessness relates to coherence, and making sense of life; isolation relates to significance, and wanting to matter; identity relates to purpose in life, and questions about 'Why am I here?'. Death, they argue, touches on all of these themes. Addressing these themes can be an important objective of psychological therapy. The voices that Margery, Julian and Joan heard addressed all of these themes and were thus epistemically therapeutic.[5] Julian's voices and visions helped her to make sense of life and gave her

---

[5] It can also be argued, of course, that Joan's voices (and Margery's to a lesser extent) were eventually harmful – bringing her into epistemic conflict with those around her. The positive meaning that Joan attributed to her voices won her friends and enemies, and the latter eventually had her killed.

courage to face death. Voices and visions gave Margery a personal sense of significance; she mattered enough that God communicated with her, and this gave her significance in the eyes of others. Joan's voices gave her a particular mission and purpose, drawing her from obscurity to political and religious significance and, eventually, the courage to face death at the stake.

The finding of meaning is a major resource for positive spiritual coping in the face of adversity and voices may play a significant part in this process. The affirmation of positive spiritual/religious coping is a much too often neglected evidence-based spiritual intervention.

3. Voices can be positive experiences

The experience of hearing voices was largely positive and affirming for each of the three women who have been at the centre of this study. Margery suffered a negative response from some of her contemporaries, although it might be argued that this had more to do with the way in which she communicated her experiences than with the experiences themselves. Julian's experience was very much one of sharing in the sufferings of Christ, and so not exactly a happy one, but nonetheless one that she treasured and reflected upon for a lifetime. Joan was executed for obedience to her voices but died believing that she had been faithful to what God, through those voices, had called her to do. The voices that Margery, Julian and Joan heard were (with a few exceptions – see below) not associated with the negative emotional valence experienced by many psychiatric patients.

Medieval voices and visions were highly positive experiences. Corinne Saunders (2016, p. 423), writing of the medieval world within which 'supernatural voices intervene', argues that there are continuities with contemporary voice hearing:

> The works of Julian and Margery open out the nature of this visionary experience, depicting its complex multi-sensory quality, its all-consuming power, its revelatory potential and profound spiritual meaning, but also the difficulties of comprehending such experience. The voices evoked in these works – internal and external; in the mind and in the soul; inspiring, instructive, protective, cautionary, forbidding, evil and tempting – continue to figure in the experiences of voice hearers.

The difference between then and now, as Saunders goes on to argue:

> lies in the ways that such voices are understood – then, as aspects of lived experience that were allowed for by the medieval world view; now, most often as symptoms of psychosis.

The possibility of having a positive experience of voice hearing, for each of these medieval women, depended first upon the spiritual significance that their voices held for them personally and second upon the wider cultural and social milieu within which it was understood and affirmed that such experiences might have theological meaning. Many voice hearers today might similarly affirm that their voices are personally meaningful but, outside of support groups such as the Hearing Voices network, or perhaps Christian churches such as those researched by Tanya Luhrmann (2012), there is much less affirmation for such experiences in the contemporary cultural and social milieu. Specifically, there is much less affirmation of such experiences within psychiatry, where they are pathologized rather than affirmed.

It is in the nature of all medical specialities to focus on signs and symptoms of disease. Psychiatry, and medicine more widely, is largely devoted to the relief of suffering. However, psychiatry also has a part to play in normalizing unusual experiences which are not signs and symptoms of disorder, and in promoting mental health. The challenge for psychiatry is to move from a place of having seen auditory verbal hallucinations almost exclusively as psychopathology to a more discriminating place of recognizing that, sometimes, voices should be affirmed as positive spiritual experiences (whether or not they are associated with a diagnosis).

4. Voices can be negative experiences

Margery and Julian did, on occasion, also hear evil voices, albeit to a much lesser degree. In Chapter 1 of her *Book*, Margery reports hearing a voice, which she identified as the devil, which variously urged her either not to confess her sins (when she might have benefitted from doing so) or else to consider herself damned and beyond forgiveness. During her puerperal illness, she heard the voices of demons that encouraged her to forsake her Christian faith. Julian, following the final revelation, heard a conversation between voices which moved her to despair, mocking her prayers. Whilst these were clearly distressing and negative experiences for these women, they would have been viewed very differently than someone hearing demonic voices today (Cook, 2020, pp. 178–83). Paradoxically, through much of Christian history up until recently, such voices were seen as evidence of holiness, after the pattern of Christ resisting the temptations of the devil in the wilderness before embarking upon his Galilean ministry (Cook, 2018, pp. 112–13, 130).

Joan never seems to have evaluated her voices as evil, but others were less sure. Apparently, positive voices may nonetheless be deceptive and misleading and, to the medieval mind, if Joan's voices were not from God, then they must have been from the devil. Needless to say, political concerns and allegiances easily influenced the judgements that Joan's contemporaries made in this respect, but the prejudicial influence of these considerations may have been less obvious then than it is to us looking back on history. England (ruled by a Norman king) and France were both Christian nations. By 1429 there was a widespread expectation that these nations would be united, and, with this union, peace achieved. Joan and her voices, now easily portrayed as saviour of France, could easily be seen in her day as an enemy of both church and state, and a threat to peace and unity. At a personal level, Joan's voices eventually brought about her death, and so we could say that they were, in the end, a very negative experience for her. Of course, it is impossible to separate such a judgement from one's view of whether the political cause was a good one or not – and this was exactly the predicament of her contemporaries and the focus of their disagreement. Did Joan die in a worthwhile cause or not?

Voices associated with mental illness today tend to have negative emotional valence (De Leede-Smith and Barkus, 2013), and this may bias our contemporary judgement as to their meaning. Such voice hearers also tend to have more passive coping strategies. Contemporary research on spiritually significant voices (most of which are not associated with mental illness and are associated with positive coping) hints at the possibility that improving coping by drawing on spiritual/religious resources may be helpful in treatment (Cook et al., 2022).

5. Diagnoses have ramifications

There has been much debate about the problems and limitations of the diagnostic paradigm within psychiatry (see, for example, Kinderman et al. (2013) and Huda (2019)). These include, amongst other things, conceptual and philosophical issues, concerns around reliability and validity, and the association of such diagnoses with stigma and prejudice. What may we learn about problems of psychiatric diagnosis, contemporary and retrospective, in relation to the three women who are the focus of the present study?

Margery was diagnosed in her lifetime as having an illness which we would almost certainly refer to as a puerperal psychosis. Margery agreed that she was not well and distinguished the spiritual experiences that she had during this illness from those that characterized her later life. Julian was recognized to have suffered a serious physical illness from which she might easily have died, but the only contemporary concern expressed about her mental state, so far as we know, was her own doubt about whether or not her experiences were simply 'ravings' associated with what we would refer to as delirium. So far as we know, no one seems to have seriously questioned Joan's mental health during her lifetime. To do so would not have been in the interests of either her allies (who believed she was inspired by God) or her enemies (who wanted to prove that she was a witch or a heretic).

Over the last century and a half, numerous retrospective diagnoses have been offered in respect of these three women, especially Margery and Joan. Some have been insightful, some tell us more about the author than the patient, some have been highly prejudicial and most have been highly speculative. Whereas a diagnosis offered by a psychiatrist, or other medical doctor, in the clinical context is usually with the intention of guiding decisions about treatment and judgements concerning prognosis, historical diagnostic exercises relating to people who died six centuries earlier are clearly differently motivated. Some may arise out of genuine historical curiosity, and a desire better to understand the significant historical figures to whom they relate. Others, whilst apparently aspiring to such aims, seem to betray ulterior motives, and are used for wholly other purposes.

The late nineteenth and early twentieth centuries saw a plethora of attempts to diagnose significant religious figures, including notably Jesus of Nazareth (Cook, 2018, pp. 82–95), as suffering from mental disorder. The earlier publications on Joan reflect this trend. The general purpose appears to have been to portray religious experiences such as visions and voices as reflective of mental ill health, and thus as signs and symptoms of mental illness in need of treatment. The underlying agenda was unashamedly atheistic albeit, we might charitably assume, with the conscious intention of improving the mental health of the population by freeing it from the shackles of unscientific ways of thinking. Ironically, since the mid-twentieth century, it has been science that has provided the evidence base to show that exactly the contrary state of affairs generally applies. That is, religious affiliation appears to be good for mental health, positive religious coping is a valuable resource for managing stress and recovering from illness and spiritual interventions may sometimes play a helpful role in mental healthcare.

In addition to an anti-religious stance, some of the diagnoses offered in respect of Margery, Julian and Joan reflect other forms of prejudice, notably misogyny and sanism (Leblanc and Kinsella, 2016). Doubtless, if our three subjects had not all been white European women, we might also have found evidence of racism. Political and nationalistic prejudices also creep in, especially in relation to Joan. Diagnosis thus easily loses the compassionate purpose for which it should only ever be employed in the clinical context and becomes instead a weapon of war in academic debate. Some might argue that this is legitimate in any historical-critical endeavour, but the danger is that these prejudices spill over into other contemporary debates about mental disorder and mental health and adversely influence both patients and clinicians in practice. Patients fear that the mental health professionals treating them will be unsympathetic to their spirituality or faith, and especially to any spiritual/religious experiences that they may have had – such as the hearing of voices. Professionals are reinforced in the fundamentally scientific epistemology of their field and fail to view things from the primarily spiritual perspective of their patient. Epistemic injustice is thus perpetuated in the clinical context.

Of course, the world in which Margery, Julian and Joan lived was very different than ours. In many ways, the opposite presumptions applied. Spiritual realities were taken for granted and there had to be particular reasons for assuming that apparently religious experiences were not just that – religious experiences. If we look back now and see this very clearly with historical perspective, then we should not be so quick to judge the medieval mindset as to question our own reverse presumptions. Why do we presume first to make diagnoses and only then to ask about spiritual concerns? When, as psychiatrists, we do make diagnoses, then what are the spiritual, social and psychological ramifications of those diagnoses? If we take care to mitigate the pharmacological side effects of treatments that we provide, do we also take care to mitigate the potentially adverse psychosocial and spiritual impact of the diagnoses that we offer?

6. Spirituality and (psychiatric) phenomenology are intertwined

The spiritualities of Margery, Julian and Joan were all Christian spiritualities, all of their time, and yet all so different. Their visionary and voice-hearing experiences are embedded within these spiritualities, shaping them and shaped by them.

Margery's conversational honesty, openness and need for affirmation conceives a spirituality within which voices and visions shape her prayers and her relationships with those around her (or – perhaps – are shaped by those prayers and relationships?) They affirm her and give her meaning and purpose. They bring healing, forgiveness, and reconciliation.

Julian's quiet, contemplative and loving search for God in the context of a life-threatening illness gives birth – through the medium of visions and voices – to a lifetime of thoughtful theological reflection, prayer, and counsel to others, as well as to one of the classic texts of Christian spirituality. Her inclusive theological vision of God's love for human beings emerges from places of death, solitude, and enclosure, but reaches out beyond these constraints – through her writing – to generations who have lived long after her.

Joan's focused, passionate and courageous obedience to the mission that her voices communicated turned the course of European history, but only after her voices had already turned the course of her own life. Joan's voices shaped her relationships with God, with the church, and with the world, but were in turn also shaped by them. Joan's voices were meaningful only within her Christian faith and worldview, but this is exactly what brought her into conflict with others who shared that faith and yet had a different political worldview.

The culturally embedded and meaningful visionary and voice-hearing experiences of these three women may seem worlds apart from a psychiatric out-patient clinic of twenty-first century Europe, dislocated as it is from any shared religious worldview. However, spirituality, whether religious or not, continues to be important for most people worldwide and even for many in the secular western world. Increasing spiritual plurality makes it more, not less, important that psychiatry should take a person-centred interest in patients' spiritualities, seeking to understand how they convey meaning, provide purpose, and shape experience. Psychopathology is both shaped by spirituality and in turn shapes spirituality. A detailed account of psychopathology, perhaps especially of visions and voices, is incomplete without an understanding of this context.

Towards a new taxonomy of spiritually significant voices

Diagnoses also form the basis for taxonomies of mental disorder, and this is important not only for the clinical context but also for epidemiological research and the promotion of public mental health (within which, spirituality has an important part to play (Cook and White, 2018)). However, the danger here is – again – that we privilege the diagnostic perspective in such a way as to perpetuate epistemic injustice. What if we put the spiritual perspective first, and then secondarily address the mental health perspective? This is not to say that we neglect diagnosis and treatment, but rather that we affirm the spiritual taxonomy over the classification of mental disorders.

In an empirical study of spiritually significant voices (Cook et al., 2022), based on a predominantly Christian sample, a provisional taxonomy was based upon a combination of frequency and context of voice hearing, affective valence and the identity of the voice (as understood by the voice hearer). Eight categories were identified:

Conversion
Calling
Crisis
Comfort
Confirming/clarifying
Communications
Conversational
Companions

Within this list, the first five categories were experienced infrequently (often only once in a lifetime) and were almost invariably positive in affective tone. As the categorical labels indicate, these voices were heavily contextual, relating to particular life circumstances, such as religious conversion, vocational calling, crisis or need for comfort or clarification in regard to important life decisions. The voice was usually identified as the voice of God (with Trinitarian variation, thus sometimes Jesus or the Holy Spirit).

The last three categories were more complex and variable. Sometimes they were infrequent, but usually more frequent. Emotional valence was sometimes positive and sometimes negative. The voice may be identified as that of God, but was sometimes identified as another spiritual being (good or evil) or as an aspect of the self (alter ego). Some of these voices arose in the course of prayer, and some were ongoing in daily life. The so-called 'communications' were messages received with wider relevance (for people other than the voice hearer). The so-called 'conversational' voices were representative of an inner dialogue. Voices referred to as 'companions' were marked out by their social agency, or sense of presence.

In this study, three quarters of respondents reported no psychiatric diagnosis, most were predominantly positive experiences, and there were hardly any overtly abusive voices. One-third reported voices that gave commands, traditionally thought to be a characteristic of voices heard in the context of mental illness, but here experienced in the absence of such diagnoses. Half of the voices in this study were experienced as arising internally, and half externally. Half were auditory, and a quarter more thought-like, with the rest being a mixture of the two.

Elsewhere, on the basis of anthropological research undertaken by Tanya Luhrmann (2011), it has been suggested that there might be three kinds of hallucinatory experiences: one associated with psychosis, one characterized by infrequent and non-distressing hallucinations ('sensory overrides') and a third – the Joan of Arc pattern – characterized by frequent and non-distressing hallucinations. Here, as with other taxonomies of voice-hearing experiences, the focus is on phenomenology and associated presence or absence of psychotic features. Some of these voices will be spiritually significant, and others will not, but it seems questionable as to whether a frequent experience of non-distressing voices would really be like those that Joan of Arc heard if lacking the spiritual/religious significance that her voices assumed.

Clearly more empirical research is needed, but what may be said in relation to the present study of Margery, Julian and Joan?

Margery's voices might be said to be primarily of the conversational kind, although with some elements of various other categories of spiritually significant voices (e.g. confirming/clarifying). If adopting Luhrmann's three-fold typology, they would have to be of the Joan of Arc pattern (frequent and non-distressing) but, in reality, they seem very different than Joan's voices in many ways (e.g. number of voices, content and context of messages conveyed).

Julian's voices would seem most like the communications category of spiritually significant voices, being infrequent, but having wider relevance for people other than the voice hearer). They also had a strongly dialogical character, but quite differently than Margery's ongoing conversational relationship with her voices in daily life. They were associated with a particular, once in a lifetime, life and death crisis. According to Luhrmann's typology we might identify them as sensory overrides.

Joan's voices, understood within the spiritually significant taxonomy, might be identified as companions, being frequently encountered in daily life, almost always positive experiences, associated with a sense of agency and presence. In Luhrmann's typology they would of course – by definition – have to be the <u>Joan of Arc pattern</u>, but strictly this categorisation depends upon whether or not one identifies other features of <u>psychosis</u>.

All of these allocations are clearly tentative and are not intended to be restrictive in any way. They are offered here more by way of stimulating further discussion than as being the last word on the matter (as if anyone could have a 'last word' in an ongoing debate such as this). We have no way of going back to interview Margery, Julian and Joan about their experiences; and although we have a surprising amount of knowledge about the phenomenology of their voices, there is clearly still so much more that we do not know. However, we do know that these were all deeply meaningful experiences; they were all spiritually significant. Despite having this in common, the experiences and contexts of these voices were also highly diverse, as were the personalities of the women who heard them. The bottom line here is not to fix any particular taxonomy of spiritually significant voices as final, but rather to highlight what history may teach us, through these women, about the diversity and contextual importance of such highly meaningful experiences.

Psychiatry and the critical medical humanities

What might we now say, in conclusion, about the place of the medical humanities in psychiatry? When I was a psychiatric trainee, my consultant gave me a subscription to a literary quarterly as a gift one Christmas and told me that literature was, for us as psychiatrists, the equivalent to what scalpels are for surgeons. How rarely since then, notwithstanding some excellent exceptions, have I found this to be appreciated within the wider world of psychiatry. I much later found myself working in a faculty of arts and humanities, exploring the human condition from the other side of the divide that has arisen in our western universities, and have come to wish that students did not have to choose so early on between the sciences and the humanities. That we have allowed these divisions to arise in the way that we have has impoverished medicine generally and psychiatry in particular. It has also resulted in a situation where much postgraduate time in university, in interdisciplinary research and education, is now spent in breaking down the very same divisions that forced these early choices upon our students in the first place.

In focusing, as we have in this book, upon the spirituality and visionary/voice-hearing experiences of three medieval women who led remarkable lives, we have also shed light upon some of the ways in which psychiatry only finds its true vocation within a broader interdisciplinary world of understanding the human condition in all its mystery and complexity. This broader world draws on insights from literature, history, philosophy, the arts and – yes – also theology and religious studies. If we treat psychiatry as only a kind of applied science, then there will always be the risk of reductionism and a loss of existential meaning. The humanities find creative and different ways of exploring those aspects of human experience which are otherwise hidden, marginalized, ineffable or invisible.[6]

An interdisciplinary research agenda and an interprofessional approach to clinical care are therefore required within which the humanities are appropriately represented. An integrated approach, within which the humanities find a place within the psychiatric curriculum, would surely be no bad thing. However, much more than this is required. The critical medical humanities move beyond attempts simply to cross boundaries in order to develop a thicker description of the human condition or an integrated and holistic approach to medical research and practice (not that these are necessarily bad things to do). Rather, it goes further, acknowledging the place of critical approaches informed by, for example, feminism, disability or post-colonial studies. It engages in a 'critical boundary-crossing in and through which new possibilities can emerge' (Whitehead and Woods, 2016, p. 8). It adopts a perspective of entanglement within which intersectionality and interdisciplinarity are prioritized over any a priori perspective of the

---

[6]This approach is central, for example, to the research aims of the Durham University Institute for Medical Humanities: https://www.durham.ac.uk/research/institutes-and-centres/medical-humanities/our-research/.

separateness of disciplines (Fitzgerald and Callard, 2015). Within these entanglements, it is proposed here, theology, spirituality and religious studies, often neglected within a secular interdisciplinary perspective, may all be located. The historical antagonisms between psychiatry and religion continue to exert their influence upon both psychiatry and theology, perpetuating the epistemic injustice that patients suffer, making it difficult for patients to seek help, and impoverishing our understanding of experiences such as voice hearing or visions. Psychological and spiritual concepts of well-being are methodologically entangled in such a way that it is almost impossible to measure one without confounding with the other and yet disciplinary silos perpetuate our unhelpful secular practices of discussing each without reference to the other, to the detriment of both patients and research.

Within this overall view of the critical medical humanities, historical perspectives, such as those explored in the present study, offer three valuable contributions (Whitehead and Woods, 2016, pp. 6–7):

1 Vantage points from which to view, reflect upon and critique the biomedical domain

2 Qualitatively different ways of critical thinking and perceiving

3 Awareness of the social and cultural processes of negotiation by way of which ideas, objects and practices come to – or disappear from – our collective attention

Margery, Julian and Joan offer us an alternative vision to that of the currently prevailing biopsychosocial model of our time, one in which spiritual and existential themes are differently prioritized and understood. This is not just a bolting on of a fourth dimension of spirituality to the existing tripartite model, but rather one within which existential meaning is thoroughly integrated into our understanding of the biological, psychological and social dimensions of the human condition. Nor is it merely an integrative exercise within which spirituality now takes a more prominent role. Rather, it is a recognition of the entanglement of transcendent and immanent perspectives, and of theology as a part of the wider tangled web of interdisciplinary understanding.

Conclusion

Spiritually significant visionary and voice-hearing experiences may take many forms. Not all of these experiences are life enhancing and enriching but many are, and even those that are not may yet be meaningful. Meaning is important to human well-being, especially at times of illness or adversity, and can play an important part in recovery from mental disorders. Why, then, has it been so neglected in clinical practice?

When a psychiatrist sees a patient who is hearing voices, these voices are very often associated with negative affective states and negative coping strategies. If the voices are spiritually significant in some way, then the spirituality or religiosity of the patient may well be entangled with the voice-hearing experience. The voices may be perceived as evil, or as carrying divine authority or perhaps even understood as evidence of demon possession. Such experiences are inherently distressing, and it is natural for the clinician to want to relieve this distress by doing all that they can to eliminate these symptoms and by offering reassurance that they are part of an illness, and not to be believed. This essentially compassionate approach to the clinical task – emphasizing relief of distress – does not, however, address the equally important need to find meaning amidst a disorientating and unsettling experience of illness. In some cases, it may even undermine the therapeutic relationship by appearing (intentionally or otherwise) to deny the spiritual worldview of the patient, a worldview which may in fact be a potentially positive coping resource.

As explored in Chapter 4, the historical entanglements (and attempted disentanglements) of psychiatry and religion, the recent debates about professional boundaries in relation to spirituality and psychiatry, the epistemic injustices associated with the hearing of spiritually significant voices in a secular society and the professional separation of the tasks of biopsychosocial care (by psychiatrists) from spiritual care (by chaplains) in most modern health services have all conspired to create a situation in which the finding of spiritual meaning is not integrally included within psychiatric treatment planning. This is a broader concern than arises simply in relation to the symptomatology of auditory verbal hallucinations; it relates to psychopathology in all domains of psychiatry, but it is brought into particular focus here.

Science has begun to recognize these issues and has begun to respond by way of appropriate methodologies to better understand the complex factors at play. Thus, for example, in an excellent article in *World Psychiatry*, Pargament and Lomax (2013) have acknowledged the 'double edged capacity of religion to enhance or damage health and well-being, particularly among psychiatric patients' (p. 26), have proposed an appropriate research agenda to address this and raised important questions concerning the implications for clinical practice. They draw on the work of the anthropologist Clifford Geertz, to argue that meaning making is the most important function of religion and affirm the promise of spiritually integrated approaches to treatment. They ask the interesting question 'Do religious and nonreligious delusions and hallucinations have a different set of etiological factors and consequences?' (p. 30). However, their five 'promising areas for further work in this domain' do not include any interdisciplinary engagement with the humanities. Their research agenda seeks to '*disentangle* the complex interplay between religion and psychopathology' (p. 30, my emphasis) not to adopt a perspective of entanglement. Only in the final few lines of their paper is there an affirmation of the need for 'the creation of respectful, collaborative relationships between psychiatry and the leaders and members of religious communities' (p. 30).

Pargament and Lomax are undoubtedly at the cutting edge of the science of spirituality and religion in relation to mental illness and we need more scientific research of the kind that they propose. However, their research agenda hardly affirms a central role to theology, religious studies or the other humanities in planning this agenda or in the revisioning of clinical care. Whilst they affirm the importance of meaning, paradoxically, one could be forgiven for thinking that it does not seem to matter too much what the meaning is. However, herein lays the problem, for patients (and psychiatrists) all have their own personal frameworks of meaning. How can a creatively entangled view of psychiatry and the humanities adequately address this enormous diversity of meaning?

Elsewhere, Pargament and Exline (2022), in a deeply insightful book on *Working with Spiritual Struggles in Psychotherapy*, explore a variety of ways in which patients struggle spiritually and affirm a positive place for addressing these struggles in psychotherapy. They devote a whole chapter to 'struggles of ultimate meaning', but really the whole book is about struggles with spiritual meaning and how to address these in psychotherapeutic practice. The patient-centred approach to psychiatry (and psychotherapy) necessarily involves working within the spiritual and theological worldview of the person seeking help, and no therapist can be an expert on all world religions or theologies. The therapist therefore cannot be an expert on any particular system of meaning, only on helping patients to find (their) meaning. However, the question still arises as to whether and how theology, religious studies and the humanities – the disciplines that grapple with meaning[1] – may contribute to the research agenda and to therapy. Are they simply 'helpmeets' (Fitzgerald and Callard, 2016, p. 35), or 'supportive friends' (Brody, 2009), or are they centrally important research partners?

My contention is that, if psychiatry is to take meaning more seriously – to become more meaningful – then it needs to recognize the 'entanglement' of the humanities with the medical sciences (including especially the neurosciences and the social sciences related to psychiatry). Going above and beyond traditional notions of interdisciplinary engagement, the concept of entanglement questions whether or not disciplinary boundaries are in fact helpful in the first place. Rather than disentangling causes, it seeks creatively to entangle, or at least to explore the inherent entanglement of, the research concerns of the humanities and the medical sciences. Fitzgerald and Callard (2016) express it in this way:

---

[1]Helen Small, for example, has defined the humanities in this way: 'The humanities study the meaning-making practices of human culture, past and present, focusing on interpretation and critical evaluation, primarily in terms of the individual response and with an ineliminable element of subjectivity' (Small, 2013, p. 23).

We are especially interested in whether the concerns, objects, methods and preoccupations of the medical humanities, not least the figure of the human at their centre, are, in fact, neatly separable or dissociable from the concerns, objects, methods and preoccupations of the medical and life sciences. And if these are – as we contend – actually not very separable at all; if the figures and preoccupations of the medical humanities are, in fact, deeply and irretrievably *entangled* in the vital, corporeal and physiological commitments of biomedicine; then, beyond well-rehearsed concessions to inter- and trans-disciplinarity, how might we more critically imagine what, exactly, a medical humanities practice is going to look like in the present century?

(pp. 35–6, original emphasis preserved)

The notion of entanglement moves beyond interdisciplinarity and integration to a more disruptive but also creative model of research and practice. It suggests a model of the critical medical humanities (and it is here that the word 'critical' distinguishes this from the traditional approach) which is:

a much more ambiguous and risky intellectual space – one willing to navigate the deep entanglements of subjectivity, experience, pathology, incorporation, and so on, which cut *across* the ways in which we understand both the human and her medicine today.

(Fitzgerald and Callard, 2016, p. 38, original emphasis preserved)

On this basis, I would propose, we need an entangling of psychiatry with the humanities. If we really believe that meaning is important to patients, it needs to be seen as important by psychiatrists too. The concerns of psychiatry (psychopathology, diagnosis, psychotherapy and so on) need to be more, not less, entangled with the concerns of the human subject as patient. This does not mean that the boundaries of good professional practice should be thrown to the wind. It does mean that psychiatry needs to be more meaningful – in a compassionate and patient-centred understanding of itself as deeply entangled with the wider human quest for meaning.

A more meaningful psychiatry might approach spiritually significant voices very differently than it has done hitherto. Moving away from a predominantly psychopathological focus, it might affirm the experience of voice hearing, and the search for meaning, as potentially highly rewarding, biographically, spiritually and in other ways (Cook, 2020). In research, genuine partnerships with the humanities would be more evident at all levels – from neuroscience to evaluating models of psychiatric training – in which there is more entangling than disentangling of human meaning making. In clinical practice, it would be more ready to engage in critical discernment of meaning through spiritual direction, spiritually integrated psychotherapy or other appropriate channels of reflection and exploration. It would surely see spiritual and religious resources as potentially valuable aids to positive coping during illness, stress and adversity, to be affirmed in treatment planning. It would similarly see spiritual struggles and other forms of 'negative' religious coping as important issues to be addressed in psychological therapies.

A more meaningful psychiatry would not necessarily abandon the task of diagnosis, which is in most circumstances a valuable aid to treatment planning and prognosis. However, it would recognize the widespread ramifications of diagnosis (both good and bad) and it would be likely to see this as just one task amongst a number of equally important tasks including, notably, the task of supporting the patient in finding meaning in their experiences. Care would be taken to ensure that a psychiatric diagnosis is not seen as inimical to meaning making and thus as contributory to epistemic injustice; if anything, it should be seen as providing all the more reason to search for meaning (insofar as this is possible) amidst disorientating disturbances of perception, affect or cognition. The idea of differential diagnosis between 'genuine' spiritual experience and mental disorder would have no place in a psychiatry concerned *both* to make medical diagnoses (where appropriate) *and* affirm the universal human search for meaning.

Our study of Margery, Julian and Joan has, I hope, contributed to this quest for a more meaningful psychiatry in various ways. I suggested in Chapter 4 that psychiatry can learn a number of things from these three figures: that voices may be meaningful, that they may support positive spiritual coping, that they may sometimes be positive experiences – but also sometimes negative experiences, that the making of diagnoses has ramifications and that spirituality and psychiatric phenomenology are intertwined. I briefly considered ways in which spiritually significant voices may be differently classified, so as to emphasis meaning and context more constructively than traditional classifications of auditory verbal hallucinations tend to do. I suggested (after Whitehead and Woods) that the historical perspective offers certain advantages in terms of critical reflection, finding different ways of thinking and perceiving and in making us more aware of the social and cultural processes of negotiation by way of which different ways of seeing things come into focus, or else are lost from sight.

At the end of this study, however, I am struck by just how entangled the hearing of spiritually significant voices is. For Margery, Julian and Joan it was inextricably entangled with medieval (Christian) theological expectations, with circumstances of suffering (war, plague and dissent), gender, sexuality and politics. For us – at least in Western Europe, in the early twenty-first century – it is surely just as deeply entangled, but in a very different, post-Christian, plural, social and cultural context within which shared systems of meaning are no longer universally affirmed and are constantly contested. This presents psychiatry with a challenge: will it get entangled with the humanities – in order that it may more meaningfully serve patients – or will it continue to attempt the futile task of trying to disentangle itself, and thus distance itself from the things that patients (and others) hold to be most meaningful?

REFERENCES

Abbott, C. (1997) His Body, the Church: Julian of Norwich's Vision of Christ Crucified. *Downside Review*, 115, 1–22.

Allen, C. (1975) The Schizophrenia of Joan of Arc. *History of Medicine*, 6, 4–7.

American Psychiatric Association (2013) *Diagnostic and Statistical Manual of Mental Disorders. Fifth Edition. DSM-5*. Washington, DC, American Psychiatric Association.

Astell, A. W. (2003) The Virgin Mary and the 'Voices' of Joan of Arc. In Astell, A. W. & Wheeler, B. (Eds) *Joan of Arc and Spirituality*. New York, Palgrave Macmillan. 37–60.

Bale, A. (2021) *Margery Kempe: A Mixed Life*. London, Reaktion Books.

Bark, N. (2002) Did Schizophrenia Change the Course of English History? The Mental Illness of Henry VI. *Medical Hypotheses*, 59, 416–21.

Barrett, W. P. (1931) *The Trial of Jeanne d'Arc*. London, Routledge.

Barstow, A. L. (1985) Joan of Arc and Female Mysticism. *Journal of Feminist Studies in Religion*, 1, 29–42.

Bauerschmidt, F. C. (1999) *Julian of Norwich and the Mystical Body Politic of Christ*. Notre Dame, University of Notre Dame.

Bayon, H. P. (1940) A Medico-Psychological Revision of the Story of Jehanne, la Pucelle de Domrémy. *Proceedings of the Royal Society of Medicine*, 34, 161–70.

Benedetto, R., Weaver, R. H., Ocker, C., Lindberg, C. & Duke, J. O. (Eds) (2008) *The New SCM Dictionary of Church History. Volume 1: From the Early Church to 1700*. London, SCM.

Bhattacharji, S. (1997) *God Is an Earthquake: The Spirituality of Margery Kempe*. London, DLT.

Bonelli, R. M. & Koenig, H. G. (2013) Mental Disorders, Religion and Spirituality 1990 to 2010: A Systematic Evidence-Based Review. *Journal of Religion and Health*, 52, 657–73.

Bremner, E. (1992) Margery Kempe and the Critics: Disempowerment and Deconstruction. In McEntire, S. J. (Ed.) *Margery Kempe: A Book of Essays*. London, Routledge. 117–35.

Brody, H. (2009) Defining the Medical Humanities: Three Conceptions and Three Narratives. *Journal of Medical Humanities*, 32, 1–7.

Burtterfield, J. & Butterfield, I. A. (1958) Joan of Arc: A Medical View. *History Today*, 8, 628–33.

Christ, C. P. (1980) *Diving Deep and Surfacing: Women Writers on Spiritual Quest*. Boston, MA, Beacon Press.

Clare, A. (1980) *Psychiatry in Dissent: Controversial Issues in Thought and Practice*. London, Routledge.

Claridge, G., Pryor, R. & Watkins, G. (1990) *Sounds from the Bell Jar: Ten Psychotic Authors*. Basingstoke, Macmillan.

Clarke, B. (1975) *Mental Disorder in Earlier Britain*. Cardiff, University of Wales Press.

Cleve, G. (1992) Margery Kempe: A Scandinavian Influence in Medieval England? In Glasscoe, M. (Ed.) *The Medieval Mystical Tradition in England: V. 1992*. Cambridge, Brewer. 163–78.

Colledge, E., Walsh, J. & Leclercq, J. (Eds) (1977) *Julian of Norwich: Showings*. New York, Paulist.

Cook, C. C. H. (2004) Addiction and Spirituality. *Addiction*, 99, 539–51.

Cook, C. C. H. (2013a) Controversies on the Place of Spirituality and Religion in Psychiatric Practice. In Cook, C. C. H. (Ed.) *Spirituality, Theology and Mental Health*. London, SCM. 1–19.

Cook, C. C. H. (2013b) *Recommendations for Psychiatrists on Spirituality and Religion*. London, Royal College of Psychiatrists.

Cook, C. C. H. (2013c) Transcendence, Immanence and Mental Health. In Cook, C. C. H. (Ed.) *Spirituality, Theology & Mental Health*. London, SCM. 141–59.

Cook, C. C. H. (2017) Spirituality and Religion in Psychiatry: The Impact of Policy. *Mental Health, Religion & Culture*, 20, 589–94.

Cook, C. C. H. (2018) *Hearing Voices, Demonic and Divine: Scientific and Theological Perspectives*. London, Routledge.

Cook, C. C. H. (2020) *Christians Hearing Voices: Affirming Experience and Finding Meaning*. London, Jessica Kingsley.

Cook, C. C. H. (2022a) Glossary. In Cook, C. C. H. & Powell, A. (Eds) *Spirituality and Psychiatry*, 2nd edn. Cambridge, Cambridge University Press. 375–400.

Cook, C. C. H. (2022b) Religion and Religious Experience. In Cook, C. C. H. & Powell, A. (Eds) *Spirituality and Psychiatry*, 2nd edn. Cambridge, Cambridge University Press. 312–31.

Cook, C. C. H. (2022c) Spirituality and Religion in Psychiatry. In Cook, C. C. H. & Powell, A. (Eds) *Spirituality and Psychiatry*, 2nd edn. Cambridge, Cambridge University Press. 1–22.

Cook, C. C. H. & Cullinan, R. J. (2022) Religious Delusions, Psychosis, and Existential Meaning in Later Life. *International Psychogeriatrics*, 1–3. doi: 10.1017/S1041610222000369

Cook, C. C. H. & Powell, A. (Eds) (2022) *Spirituality & Psychiatry*. Cambridge, Cambridge University Press.

Cook, C. C. H., Powell, A., Alderson-Day, B. & Woods, A. (2022) Hearing Spiritually Significant Voices: A Phenomenological Survey and Taxonomy. *BMJ Medical Humanities*, 48, 273–84.

Cook, C. C. H. & White, N. H. (2018) Resilience and the Role of Spirituality. In Bhugra, D., Bhui, K., Yeung, S., Wong, S. & Gilman, S. E. (Eds) *Oxford Textbook of Public Mental Health*. Oxford, Oxford University Press. 513–20.

Craig, L. A. (2014) The History of Madness and Mental Illness in the Middle Ages: Directions and Questions. *History Compass*, 12, 729–44.

Craun, M. (2005) The Story of Margery Kempe. *Psychiatric Services*, 56, 655–6.

Crichton, P., Carel, H. & Kidd, I. J. (2017) Epistemic Injustice in Psychiatry. *BJPsych Bulletin*, 41, 65–70.

Cross, F. L. & Livingstone, E. A. (2005) *The Oxford Dictionary of the Christian Church*. Oxford, Oxford University Press.

Culliford, L. (2011) *The Psychology of Spirituality*. London, Jessica Kingsley.

d'Orsi, G. & Tinuper, P. (2006) 'I Heard Voices …': From Semiology, a Historical Review, and a New Hypothesis on the Presumed Epilepsy of Joan of Arc. *Epilepsy & Behavior*, 9, 152–7.

d'Orsi, G. & Tinuper, P. (2016) The 'Voices' of Joan of Arc and Epilepsy with Auditory Features. *Epilepsy & Behaviour*, 61, 281.

Datta, V. (2016) Humanities More Important Than Ever in the Era of Scientific Psychiatry. *American Journal of Psychiatry Residents' Journal*, 11, 2.

Davies, O. (1992) Transformational Processes in the Work of Julian of Norwich and Mechthild of Magdeburg. In Glasscoe, M. (Ed.) *The Medieval Mystical Tradition in England: V. 1992*. Cambridge, Brewer. 39–52.

de Leede-Smith, S. & Barkus, E. (2013) A Comprehensive Review of Auditory Verbal Hallucinations: Lifetime Prevalence, Correlates and Mechanisms in Healthy and Clinical Individuals. *Frontiers in Human Neuroscience*, 7, 367.

de Menezes, A. & Moreira-Almeida, A. (2009) Differential Diagnosis between Spiritual Experiences and Mental Disorders of Religious Content. *Revista de Psiquiatria Clinica*, 36, 69–76.

de Toffol, B. (2016) Comment on 'Joan of Arc: Sanctity, Witchcraft, or Epilepsy?'. *Epilepsy & Behaviour*, 61, 80–1.

Dein, S. & Cook, C. C. H. (2015) God Put a Thought into My Mind: The Charismatic Christian Experience of Receiving Communications from God. *Mental Health, Religion & Culture*, 18, 97–113.

Devries, K. (2003) Joan of Arc's Call to Crusade. In Astell, A. W. & Wheeler, B. (Eds) *Joan of Arc and Spirituality*. New York, Palgrave Macmillan. 111–26.

Doob, P. B. R. (1974) *Nebuchadnezzar's Children: Conventions of Madness in Middle English Literature*. New Haven, Yale University Press.

Dosani, S. (2021) The Value and Benefit of Narrative Medicine for Psychiatric Practice. *BJPsych Bulletin*, 45, 274–6.

Drucker, T. (1972) Malaise of Margery Kempe. *New York State Journal of Medicine*, 72, 2911–17.

Feiss, H. (2004) Dilation: God and the World in the Visions of Benedict and Julian of Norwich. *The American Benedictine Review*, 55, 55–73.

Fitzgerald, D. & Callard, F. (2015) Social Science and Neuroscience beyond Interdisciplinarity: Experimental Entanglements. *Theory Culture & Society*, 32, 3–32.

Fitzgerald, D. & Callard, F. (2016) Entangling the Medical Humanities. In Whitehead, A., Woods, A., Atkinson, S., Macnaughton, J. & Richards, J. (Eds) *The Edinburgh Companion to the Critical Medical Humanities*. Edinburgh, Edinburgh University Press. 35–49.

Foote-Smith, E. & Bayne, L. (1991) Joan of Arc. *Epilepsia*, 32, 810–15.

Fraioli, D. (2003) Gerson Judging Women of Spirit: From Female Mystics to Joan of Arc. In Astell, A. W. & Wheeler, B. (Eds) *Joan of Arc and Spirituality*. New York, Palgrave Macmillan. 147–65.

Freeman, P. R., Bogarad, C. R. & Sholomskas, D. E. (1990) Margery Kempe, a New Theory: The Inadequacy of Hysteria and Postpartum Psychosis as Diagnostic Categories. *History of Psychiatry*, 1, 169–90.

Gaucher, G., Conroy, S. & Dwyer, D. J. (Eds) (2008) *The Plays of St Thérèse of Lisieux*. Washington, DC, Institute of Carmelite Studies.

Gillespie, V. & Ross, M. (1992) The Apophatic Image: The Poetics of Effacement in Julian of Norwich. In Glasscoe, M. (Ed.) *The Medieval Mystical Tradition in England: V. 1992*. Cambridge, Brewer. 53–77.

Gillespie, V. & Ross, M. (2004) 'With Mekeness Aske Perseverantly': On Reading Julian of Norwich. *Mystics Quarterly*, 30, 126–41.

Henderson, D. K. (1939) *Psychopathic States*. New York, Norton.

Henker, F. O. (1984) Joan of Arc and DSM III. *Southern Medical Journal*, 77, 1488–90.

Hobbins, D. (Ed.) (2005) *The Trial of Joan of Arc*. Cambridge, MA, Harvard University Press.

Huda, A. S. (2019) *The Medical Model in Mental Health: An Explanation and Evaluation*. Oxford, Oxford University Press.

Hurst, L. C. (1982) Porphyria Revisited. *Medical History*, 26, 179–82.

Inge, W. R. (1906) *Studies of English Mystics. St Margaret's Lectures 1905*. London, Murray.

Ireland, W. W. (1883) On the Character and Hallucinations of Joan of Arc. *Journal of Mental Science*, 29, 18–26.

Ireland, W. W. (1885) *The Blot Upon the Brain: Studies in History and Psychology*. Edinburgh, Bell & Bradfute.

Jacob, K. S. (2015) Recovery Model of Mental Illness: A Complementary Approach to Psychiatric Care. *Indian Journal of Psychological Medicine*, 37, 117–19.

Jacobson, A. C. (1917) The Case of Joan of Arc: Was the Maid Insane? *The Medical Times*, 45, 163–5.

James, G. W. B. (1930) Psychiatry and History. *Cambridge University Medical Society Magazine*, 34, 3–18.

Jantzen, G. (2000) *Julian of Norwich*. London, SPCK.

Jefferies, D. & Horsfall, D. (2014) Forged by Fire: Margery Kempe's Account of Postnatal Psychosis. *Literature and Medicine*, 32, 348–64.

Jutel, A. & Russell, G. (2021) Past, Present and Imaginary: Pathography in All Its Forms. *Health (London)*, 1–17. DOI: 10.1177/13634593211060759.

Kalas, L. (2020) *Margery Kempe's Spiritual Medicine: Suffering, Transformation and the Life-Course*. Cambridge, D.S. Brewer.

Kamtchum-Tatuene, J. & Fogang, Y. (2016) Comment on 'Joan of Arc: Sanctity, Witchcraft or Epilepsy?'. *Epilepsy & Behaviour*, 58, 137–8.

Kelly, H. A. (2003) Saint Joan and Confession: Internal and External Forum. In Astell, A. W. & Wheeler, B. (Eds) *Joan of Arc and Spirituality*. New York, Palgrave Macmillan. 61–84.

Kelly, H. A. (2014) Joan of Arc's Last Trial: The Attack of the Devil's Advocates. In Wheeler, B. & Wood, C. T. (Eds) *Fresh Verdicts on Joan of Arc*. New York, Routledge. 205–36.

Kenyon, F. E. (1971) The Life and Health of Joan of Arc: An Exercise in Pathography. *The Practitioner*, 207, 835–42.

Kenyon, F. E. (1973) Pathography and Psychiatry. *Canadian Psychiatric Association Journal*, 18, 63–6.

Kidd, I. J., Spencer, L. & Carel, H. (2022) Epistemic Injustice in Psychiatric Research and Practice. *Philosophical Psychology*, 1–29.

Kieckhefer, R. (1988) Major Currents in Late Medieval Devotion. In Raitt, J., Mcginn, B. & Meyendorff, J. (Eds) *Christian Spirituality: High Middle Ages and Reformation*. London, SCM. 75–108.

Kinderman, P., Read, J., Moncrieff, J. & Bentall, R. P. (2013) Drop the Language of Disorder. *Evidence Based Mental Health*, 16, 2–3.

Koenig, H. G. (2008) Concerns about Measuring 'Spirituality' in Research. *Journal of Nervous and Mental Disease*, 196, 349–55.

Koenig, H. G. (2018) *Religion and Mental Health: Research and Clinical Applications*. London, Academic Press.

Kuhn, C. C. (1988) A Spiritual Inventory of the Medically Ill Patient. *Psychiatric Medicine*, 6, 87–100.

Lawes, R. (1999) The Madness of Margery Kempe. In Glasscoe, M. (Ed.) *The Medieval Mystical Tradition. Exeter Symposium VI.* Woodbridge, Brewer. 147–67.

Leamy, M., Bird, V., Le Boutillier, C., Williams, J. & Slade, M. (2011) Conceptual Framework for Personal Recovery in Mental Health: Systematic Review and Narrative Synthesis. *British Journal of Psychiatry*, 199, 445–52.

Leblanc, S. & Kinsella, E. A. (2016) Toward Epistemic Justice: A Critically Reflexive Examination of 'Sanism' and Implications for Knowledge Generation. *Studies in Social Justice*, 10, 59–78.

Luhrmann, T. M. (2000) *Of Two Minds: The Growing Disorder in American Psychiatry.* New York, Knopf.

Luhrmann, T. M. (2011) Hallucinations and Sensory Overrides. *Annual Review of Anthropology*, 40, 71–85.

Luhrmann, T. M. (2012) *When God Talks Back.* New York, Knopf.

Maclaurin, C. (1919) Jeanne d'Arc as a Pathological Study. *The Medical Journal of Australia*, 1, 255–7.

Macmin, L. & Foskett, J. (2004) 'Don't Be Afraid to Tell.' The Spiritual and Religious Experience of Mental Health Service Users in Somerset. *Mental Health, Religion & Culture*, 7, 23–40.

Mazour-Matusevich (2003) A Reconsideration of Jean Gerson's Attitude toward Joan of Arc in Light of His Views on Popular Devotion. In Astell, A. W. & Wheeler, B. (Eds) *Joan of Arc and Spirituality.* New York, Palgrave Macmillan. 167–82.

McConnell, H. H. (1993) From Shame to Joy: Julian of Norwich, Companion on the Journey to Spiritual Wellness. *Studies in Formative Spirituality*, 14, 395–405.

McEntire, S. J. (1992a) The Journey into Selfhood: Margery Kempe and Feminine Spirituality. In McEntire, S. J. (Ed.) *Margery Kempe: A Book of Essays.* London, Routledge. 51–69.

McEntire, S. J. (Ed.) (1992b) *Margery Kempe: A Book of Essays.* London, Routledge.

McIlwain, J. T. (1984) The 'Bodelye Syeknes' of Julian of Norwich. *Journal of Medieval History*, 10, 167–80.

Medcalf, S. (1981) Inner and Outer. In Medcalf, S. (Ed.) *The Later Middle Ages.* London, Methuen. 108–71.

Meech, S. B. & Allen, H. E. (Eds) (1940) *The Book of Margery Kempe. The Text from the Unique Ms. Owned by Colonel W. Butler-Bowden. Vol. I.* Oxford, Oxford University Press.

Merton, T. (1967) *Mystics and Zen Masters.* New York, Noonday Press.

Mitchell, P. D. (2011) Retrospective Diagnosis and the Use of Historical Texts for Investigating Disease in the Past. *International Journal of Paleopathology*, 1, 81–8.

Molinari, P. (1958) *Julian of Norwich: The Teaching of a 14th Century English Mystic*. London, Longmans, Green & Co.

Money-Kyrle, R. (1933) A Psycho-Analytic Study of the Voices of Joan of Arc. *British Journal of Medical Psychology*, 13, 63–81.

Muhammed, L. (2013) A Retrospective Diagnosis of Epilepsy in Three Historical Figures: St Paul, Joan of Arc and Socrates. *Journal of Medical Biography*, 21, 208–11.

Mursell, G. (2001) *English Spirituality: From Earliest Times to 1700*. London, SPCK.

Nash-Marshall, S. (1999) *Joan of Arc: A Spiritual Biography*. New York, Crossroad.

Nicastro, N. & Picard, F. (2016) Joan of Arc: Sanctity, Witchcraft or Epilepsy? *Epilepsy & Behaviour*, 57, 247–50.

Nores, J. M. & Yakovleff, Y. (1995) A Historical Case of Disseminated Chronic Tuberculosis. *Neuropsychobiology*, 32, 79–80.

Ober, W. B. (1985) Margery Kempe: Hysteria and Mysticism Reconciled. *Literature and Medicine*, 4, 24–40.

Ouwehand, E. (2020) Mania and Meaning. A Mixed Methods Study into Religious Experiences in People with Bipolar Disorder: Occurrence and Significance. *Faculty of Theology & Religious Studies*. Groningen, University of Groningen.

Ouwehand, E., Muthert, H., Zock, H., Boeije, H. & Braam, A. (2018) Sweet Delight and Endless Night: A Qualitative Exploration of Ordinary and Extraordinary Religious and Spiritual Experiences in Bipolar Disorder. *The International Journal for the Psychology of Religion*, 28, 31–54.

Pargament, K. I. & Exline, J. J. (2022) *Working with Spiritual Struggles in Psychotherapy*. New York, Guilford Press.

Pargament, K. I. & Lomax, J. W. (2013) Understanding and Addressing Religion among People with Mental Illness. *World Psychiatry*, 12, 26–32.

Pattison, S. (2007) Absent Friends in Medical Humanities. *Medical Humanities*, 33, 65–6.

Payne, S. (1993) Simplicity. In Downey, M. (Ed.) *The New Dictionary of Catholic Spirituality*. Collegeville, Liturgical Press. 885–9.

Payne, S. (2005) Simplicity. In Sheldrake, P. (Ed.) *The New SCM Dictionary of Christian Spirituality*. London, SCM. 583–4.

Pelphrey, B. (1989) *Christ Our Mother: Julian of Norwich*. London, DLT.

Pepler, C. (1958) *The English Religious Heritage*. St Louis, Herder.

Pernoud, R. (1964) *Joan of Arc: By Herself and Her Witnesses*. London, Macdonald.

Person-Centred Training and Curriculum (PCTC) Scoping Group & Special Committee on Professional Practice and Ethics (2018) Person-Centred Care: Implications for Training in Psychiatry. *College Report*. London, Royal College of Psychiatrists.

Peters, B. (2008) Julian of Norwich's Showings and The Ancrene Riwle: Two Rhetorical Configurations of Mysticism. *Rhetoric Review*, 27, 361–78.

Pinzino, J. M. (2003) Joan of Arc and *Lex Privata*: A Spirit of Freedom in the Law. In Astell, A. W. & Wheeler, B. (Eds) *Joan of Arc and Spirituality*. New York, Palgrave Macmillan. 85–109.

Poole, R. & Higgo, R. (2011) Spirituality and the Threat to Therapeutic Boundaries in Psychiatric Practice. *Mental Health, Religion & Culture*, 14, 19–29.

Porter, R. (1996) *A Social History of Madness: Stories of the Insane*. London, Phoenix.

Raitt, J., Mcginn, B. & Meyendorff, J. (Eds) (1988) *Christian Spirituality: II. High Middle Ages and Reformation*. London, SCM.

Ramirez, J. (2017) *Julian of Norwich: A Very Brief History*. London, SPCK.

Ratnasuriya, R. H. (1986) Joan of Arc, Creative Psychopath: Is There Another Explanation? *Journal of the Royal Society of Medicine*, 79, 234–5.

Riehle, W. (2014) *The Secret Within: Hermits, Recluses, and Spiritual Outsiders in Medieval England*. Ithaca, Cornell University Press.

Robb, J., Cessford, C., Dittmar, J., Inskip, S. A. & Mitchell, P. D. (2021) The Greatest Health Problem of the Middle Ages? Estimating the Burden of Disease in Medieval England. *International Journal of Paleopathology*, 34, 101–12.

Rosmarin, D. H. & Koenig, H. G. (Eds) (2020) *Handbook of Spirituality, Religion and Mental Health*. London, Academic Press.

Ross, M. (1993) Apophatic Prayer as a Theological Model: Seeking Coordinates in the Ineffable. Notes for a Quantum Theology. *Journal of Literature and Theology*, 7, 325–53.

Ross, M. (2013) Behold Not the Cloud of Experience. In Jones, E. A. (Ed.) *The Medieval Mystical Tradition in England. Exeter Symposium VIII*. Cambridge, Brewer. 29–50.

Ross, M. (2014) *Silence: A User's Guide*. Eugene, Cascade.

Russell, D. (2013) Religious Mystical Mothers: Margery Kempe and Caterina Benincasa. In Jones, E. A. (Ed.) *The Medieval Mystical Tradition in England. Exeter Symposium VIII*. Cambridge, Brewer. 75–92.

Saadeh, M. G., North, K., Hansen, K. L., Steele, P. & Peteet, J. R. (2018) Spiritual Direction and Psychotherapy. *Spirituality in Clinical Practice*, 5, 273–82.

Saunders, C. (2016) Voices and Visions: Mind, Body and Affect in Medieval Writing. In Whitehead, A., Woods, A., Atkinson, S., Macnaughton, J. & Richards, J. (Eds) *The Edinburgh Companion to the Critical Medical Humanities*. Edinburgh, Edinburgh University Press. 411–27.

Savage, A., Watson, N. & Ward, B. (Eds) (1991) *Anchoritic Spirituality: Ancrene Wisse and Associated Works*. New York, Paulist.

Schlozman, S. C. (2017) Why Psychiatric Education Needs the Humanities. *Academic Psychiatry*, 41, 703–6.

Searle, W. (1976) *The Saint & the Skeptics: Joan of Arc in the Work of Mark Twain, Anatole France, and Bernard Shaw*. Detroit, Wayne State University.

Sherley-Price, L. (1988) *The Ladder of Perfection*. London, Penguin.

Shorter, E. (2005) *A Historical Dictionary of Psychiatry*. Oxford, Oxford University Press.

Small, H. (2013) *The Value of the Humanities*. Oxford, Oxford University Press.

Stephens, W. (Ed.) (1925) *The Life of Joan of Arc by Anatole France*. London, The Bodley Head.

Sullivan, K. (1999) *The Interrogation of Joan of Arc*. Minneapolis, University of Minnessota.

Sullivan, K. (2014) 'I Do Not Name to You the Voice of St Michael': The Identification of Joan of Arc's Voices. In Wheeler, B. & Wood, C. T. (Eds) *Fresh Verdicts on Joan of Arc*. New York, Routledge. 85–111.

Tavard, G. H. (1997) The Spirituality of St Joan. In Tallon, M. E. (Ed.) *Joan of Arc at the University*. Milwaukee, Marquette University Press. 43–58.

Tavard, G. H. (1998) *The Spiritual Way of St. Jeanne d'Arc*. Collegeville, Michael Glazier.

Taylor, C. (Ed.) (2006) *Joan of Arc: La Pucelle*. Manchester, Manchester University Press.

Thouless, R. H. (1924) *The Lady Julian: A Psychological Study*. London, SPCK.

Thurston, H. (1936) Margery the Astonishing: A Fifteenth-Century English Mystic. *The Month*, 446–56.

Torn, A. (2008) Margery Kempe: Madwoman or Mystic – a Narrative Approach to the Representation of Madness and Mysticism in Medieval England. *Narrative and Fiction: An Interdisciplinary Approach*. Huddersfield, University of Huddersfield. 79–89.

Trenery, C. & Horden, P. (2017) Madness in the Middle Ages. In Eghigian, G. (Ed.) *The Routledge History of Madness and Mental Health*. London, Routledge. 62–80.

Van Tongeren, D. R. & Showalter Van Tongeren, S. A. (2020) *The Courage to Suffer: A New Clinical Framework for Life's Greatest Crises*. West Conshohocken, PA, Templeton.

Ward, B. (1988) Julian the Solitary. In Llewelyn, R. (Ed.) *Julian Reconsidered*. Oxford, SLG Press. 11–31.

Warner, M. (2013) *Joan of Arc: The Image of Female Heroism*. Oxford, Oxford University Press.

Whitehead, A. & Woods, A. (2016) Introduction. In Whitehead, A., Woods, A., Atkinson, S., Macnaughton, J. & Richards, J. (Eds) *The Edinburgh Companion to the Critical Medical Humanities*. Edinburgh, Edinburgh University Press. 1–31.

Wiethaus, U. (2005) Christian Spirituality in the Medieval West (600–1450). In Holder, A. (Ed.) *The Blackwell Companion to Christian Spirituality*. Oxford, Blackwell. 106–21.

Williams, R. (2014) *The Anti-Theology of Julian of Norwich*. Norwich, The Friends of Julian of Norwich.

Windeatt, B. A. (Ed.) (1994) *The Book of Margery Kempe*. London, Penguin.

Wolters, C. (1966) *Julian of Norwich: Revelations of Divine Love*. London, Penguin.

INDEX